Half My Life
How Jesus Conquered My Soul

Thomas Murosky, PhD

© 2021 by Thomas Murosky, Ph.D.

Published by Our Walk in Christ Publishing
State College, PA
www.owicpub.com

All rights reserved. No part of this publication may be reproduced, distributed, or transmitted in any form or by any means, including photocopying, recording, or other electronic or mechanical methods, without the prior written permission of the publisher, except in the case of brief quotations embodied in critical reviews and certain other noncommercial uses permitted by copyright law.

Half My Life: How Jesus Conquered My Soul

First Printing 2021
ISBN: 978-1-7348398-2-1 (sc)
ISBN: 978-1-7348398-3-8 (e)

Scripture quotations taken from the New American Standard Bible® (NASB), Copyright © 1960, 1962, 1963, 1968, 1971, 1972, 1973, 1975, 1977, 1995 by The Lockman Foundation. Used by permission. www.lockman.org

The Internet addresses in this book are accurate at the time of publication. They are provided as a resource, but due to the nature of the Internet, those addresses may change.

Commitment to Open Source: Our Walk in Christ Publishing uses FOSS software where available. This book was produced with LibreOffice, GNU Image Manipulator Program, Sigil, Calibre, and the following open fonts: Abhaya Libre, Afta Sans, and Dancing Script. Audiobook edition produced with Audacity and Kid3.

Library of Congress Control Number: 2021946229

Table of Contents

Index of Poetry...4
A Brief Word..6
Introduction..9
Seeds of Destruction..13
    Am I Alone?..15
    Mommy, Who is God?..23
    Who's My Daddy?...29
    Can I Have That?...39
    Can You Keep a Secret?...47
One Wicked Sapling...55
    Is There a Friend for Me?...57
    Your Child's Worst Influence..69
    No Family Man..79
    I Don't Care If I Go to Heaven...89
    Empty Pleasure in Myself..95
A Journey Down the Wide Road..99
    Father Knows Nothing...101
    Academic Excellence..111
    Learning to Hate the World..121
    I Hate Feeling So Good...135
    Who Needs Your Useless God...145
Interlude: The Hound of Heaven..151
Sin's Stronghold..159
    Losing All Respect..161
    Suicidal Tendencies..167
    Paranoid in the Upper Room..173
    Pridefully Successful..181
    Who Are You, Dad?...185
    Times with a Temptress..191
    Smarter Than the Average Christian......................................199
    The Filthy Drink..203
    Brush With Mortality..209
Found by Jesus..215
    The Time Has Come..217
    Be Ye Sanctified..227
    A Worker Approved..237
    Miracles and Prophecies...247
    Though You Slay Me...257
    A Tale of Two Lifestyles...263
Scripture Index...271

Index of Poetry

- Flowing Times 52
- Solitude 67
- Leech 68
- Mother 76
- Ashes to Ashes, Dust to Dust 2 109
- Beliefs 118
- Lost Silent Demise 130
- Ashes to Ashes, Dust to Dust 140
- Demons 141
- February's Dream 165
- Footsteps 178
- Father 188
- A Dreamers Man in a Dreamers Land 198
- White Washed heart 223
- Temptations 234
- No Love 235
- The Sower in the Garden 244

Dedication

I wish to dedicate this book to those first human agents whom, first unbeknownst to me, started praying for me prior to Christ redeeming my soul. Billy, Jeremy, Brett, Rhonda, David, and their respective churches.

I also wish to acknowledge my biological father, John Murosky, who passed away during the writing of this manuscript.

A Brief Word

My life story will be difficult for me to write as well as for my readers to comprehend. So, before I start, I want to say a few things.

First, I do not mean any offense to any old family or friends. I will be telling my story as it was handed to me by my God. I trust that by telling my story to the best of my memory, and with honesty to the facts I have uncovered about my life, it will help someone out there see who God really is. I want to show how He works and maybe how to learn to trust Him more. This story is not embellished, and will be factually correct to all my available memory and resources. I do not hold any of my past against any of my family, and often, their reactions were the results of how they were treated as they grew up. I was freed from repeating the sins of my fathers when I found a God with the power to break the dysfunctional cycles in my family.

Second, I have changed the names of people throughout this book.

Third, through this story I am not looking for any pity or sympathy. I believe our present culture likes to play the 'victim' card too much and seeks to gain advantage through pity. That is not my intention, in fact, I want to do the opposite. If I am able to come from where I did, reject the worldly ways, and find peace in my own life, I believe that everyone can do the same. My message for my readers is to stop using past traumas as an excuse and instead, take any action you can to better your life today.

Finally, I have decided to intersperse the chapters with my poetry that was written most in my teenage life. The poems were my explanation of life. Sometimes they held worldviews different than I hold now, but they often reflected my past. They were written as a high school and college youth, and I have chosen not to edit them outside of basic spelling errors. Some of them are genuinely great poems, sometimes they are included for their significance to the portion of my life for which they appear.

> He will die for lack of instruction,
> And in the greatness of his folly he will go astray.
> *Proverbs 5:23*

Introduction

I was conceived on a boat in the middle of Lake Erie. Everybody on board was drunk, and my life went downhill from there. I know this story because it was often relayed to me in anger when certain discussions about 'that man' occurred. My mom was not much for subtlety about her feelings toward 'the jerk', I mean, Dad, but we'll talk more about that later.

As for my mom, she did what she could given her circumstances. She always worked to pay the bills, to keep my brother and me fed, and even to provide some pleasures in life. But there were struggles in the home with her domineering second husband. With her street smarts, she had the know-how to leave everything behind to protect herself and her children. On that horribly confusing day for my five-year-old self, she secured passage across the United States with a Vietnam war veteran-turned hippie, two children in tow, to start life anew. It was not always easy, but she saw that our physical needs were provided for.

Provision for our emotional needs, however, was lacking. I grew up as an isolated child, always the punchline to the joke at home and school. I guess I was just irresistibly easy to tease. Maybe it was my bad social mannerisms, or the way I would dress myself every morning. Perhaps it was my inability to hold–let alone throw–a football, or the curious ways I would try to be like the other kids. Perhaps I was teased for no other reason than to be the god-given pinata to the cruel offspring of the local socialites.

Introduction

In my formative years, Mom was nearly always at work or asleep. I only remember a few times of playing games with her, doing activities, or just being a family together. This wasn't her fault. Anytime a child is being raised by a single mother, there is a tug-o'-war with the world: make the money or spend time with the kids. My mom made the money, not for greed, but necessity. There were bills to pay and no man in the family to help. Us kids were on our own, either being raised at a day care or at a crazy sitter's house. Later on, but still too early for our youthful lusts, we were left to raise ourselves.

As kids exploring the world alone, our dominion became the woods as we mastered the trails, built forts, and did battle with the creatures of our wild imaginations. Because I was the younger of two, I became an isolated child reducing 'we' to myself and my imagination. Eventually I would make some friends, but they were few and far between, and often they would lead my untempered life into dangerous realms of sexuality, conflict with the law, or even depression.

With no boundaries or direction in life, I found myself in places where no child should be found. I had never before read the phrase, w*here there is no vision, the people are unrestrained*[1], but before I was ten years old, I was a hoodlum: a thief, a smoker, and a sex fiend. What could cause such rapid descent into a chain of self-destructive behavior? In my story, we will find out how I started looking for God in all the wrong places, and how He, ultimately, found me.

It is true that I poked and probed at every religion I could find in my exploratory teenage years. That is to say, I explored every religion except Christianity! I ignored that one religion with the ferocious voracity that could only come from a battered child of the world. But after a long period of fighting with God

---

[1] Proverbs 29:18

Introduction

and the world, Jesus Christ eventually conquered me at the ripe age of about twenty. He came in and showed me how my destructive behavior caused my isolation, and how my isolation encouraged that behavior. I had no resistance left. When the encounter with Christ occurred one cold January day, all the remorse over my past deeds oozed out of my body in a twelve-hour stream of tears. I immediately saw changes in my wretched soul. And God had only begun this work in me.

This testimony will illustrate the horrible consequences of a young life untouched by discipline, how a fatherless child met his real Daddy, and how I had to break down my entire life's presuppositions and rebuild myself on a new foundation.

Herein, I tell the story of how I turned my heart away from darkness and toward the glorious light of my Lord and Savior, Jesus Christ. I hope that my story will inspire you to seek out a journey with God and that He reaches you in the same way He reached me.

Seeds of Destruction

They conceive mischief and bring forth iniquity,
And their mind prepares deception.
Job 15:35

Am I Alone?

Do our earliest memories have rhyme or reason in the ways they pierce the darkness of our youth and embed themselves in our minds? I ponder this question as I look back to my first memory fragments and wonder if they hold any meaning. Sometimes I grasp for reasons for these memories, but often I cannot spot the significance until replaying all my memories with the benefit of hindsight.

When I was a toddler, we moved out west where some of my earliest memories fixed themselves in my mind. I recall sitting on an old discarded couch cushion, probably infested with some insect larvae; most likely the same cockroaches which infested our new home. On this dirty, padded perch, I watched the older kids riding their bikes. Their huge eight-year-old bodies were the envy of my tiny frame as I wished I could join them in play. Perhaps this early memory is the reflection of the lonely life I was destined to endure.

It was not that I didn't desire loneliness. I often sought it. Perhaps it was the silence of being alone that I desired. Our home was many things, but quiet was not one of them. The first few months of living with Mom's boyfriend, whom we called 'Dad', were fabulous. This was the honeymoon stage as sociologists call it. But the honeymoon ended, and the true colors of two radically dysfunctional people blended with all the elegance of water and oil.

I had never heard the term 'vicarious abuse' until many years later, but I was plunged into it, like a child learning in submersion education. I, however, learned the language of emotional suppression. Daddy would come home around 5:30 every night, and he was the delight of my life. To us kids, he was always gentle, loving, and caring. But to Mom, he was a tyrant; abusive and vulgar. The fights wouldn't break out until after bedtime, but once they did, angry noises penetrated the silent sanctuary of our bedroom. In an effort to drown out the noise, I began what child psychologists call headbanging but what we referred to around the house as 'La Las'. This phase usually comes upon a child like a mist, here one day, gone soon after. When a young child has fear or conflict, the phase becomes a habit and digs in deep for the long haul. I made it to adulthood before I finally overpowered this long-held habit that burrowed itself into me from the yelling that persisted night after night.

I sought solitude to balance the angry noises I heard night after night. Once I glimpsed a small taste of freedom, I took it for all it was worth. What did Thoreau say? "I want to live deep and suck all the marrow out of life." My first taste of such freedom arrived in our early morning rituals.

Mom and Dad left for work before we were off; I to the babysitter's house before my afternoon kindergarten class, and my brother to the second grade. We dressed ourselves—or at least tried to. I always put on my new underwear, but no one told me I had to take off the old pair first!

We watched our morning cartoon shows like a smoker must inhale before the long shift, and then my brother headed off to school in time to catch the 7:55 bus. I had five minutes to get across the walkway to the sitter's house. While I always made my deadline, I rarely went in during the morning check-in. I would knock on the door every day and ask to go to Brandon's house. He lived in our complex, down past the pool. He was my age and his older brother was my brother's best friend.

While I knew Brandon, he was not a friend as much as an opportune playmate while we were at their house. I had nothing against him, it is just that at five years old, we don't generally have the capacity to understand the relationship of "friends". Still, I asked to go to his house every day, but I only ever knocked on the door a few times. I knew he wasn't there, he had early kindergarten like everyone else in my complex who was my age. So I roamed between the apartment buildings alone, being sure not to pass by the windows of the sitter's house. I explored every bit of the complex, enjoying my time alone. I forsook the snacks and company I would have to pursue silence instead[1].

I was noticed in more positive ways at school by the nice teachers and the kids in class. It was one of the places I enjoyed because of the kids my age there, though I didn't live close to any of them. I only had two childhood playmates in our apartment complex. I already mentioned Brandon, who was the first, but the other lived directly under our apartment.

I remember preschool with my neighbor, but when we went off to kindergarten, we were separated. While I was the only one in the complex who attended the afternoon class, the kids I met at school brightened my day. Going to school made me feel like a 'big boy,' and so I looked forward to my daily routine of solitude in the morning, friends in the afternoon, back to the sitter's house for an hour after school, then home with the family.

While I was too young to recognize the in-home interactions as abuse, I heard it night after night, becoming desensitized to the yelling. It was so bad that my mom worked on several exit

---
1   Proverbs 17·1

strategies. These momentary escapes resembled confusing vacations in my immature mind. Mom looked to men to get her out of our circumstances, whether it was my biological father, her current boyfriend, or even strange men she would meet at her job as a keno runner in the Nevada casinos. We would come home on the occasional Friday after school, collect a few essential belongings, and go stay with guys out in the desert. There were a few of these events, but Dad always found us to bring us home.

One day, however, Mom planned to leave in a way that Dad couldn't find us. It all started with the normal daily routine. I wandered the complex for the last time, went to preschool, and got off the bus with my brother at the edge of a construction zone, which had become our frequent playground. We checked in with the babysitter, and when we knocked on the door that late February day, we were surprised when Mom opened it up.

Our joy was short-lived. After hugs, she quickly ushered us up to the apartment where she took the pillowcases off our pillows and handed one of them to us, telling us to fit as much as we could into it. We grabbed Legos, GoBots, and a few other trinkets while mom filled the other case with just enough clothes for a few days. Most of the toys in that bag were joint ownership with my brother. The only two belongings that were my own was my Garfield baseball cap and my Goodnight Carebear. With our few items collected, we walked out of the apartment and back to the sitter's house where we met a new stranger whom we called 'Turk'.

My brother went to say goodbye to his best friend, but I wasn't permitted to say goodbye to anyone. I wanted to go say goodbye to Brandon, even though he was not a real good friend, but just because my older brother was going over there. Upon my brother's quick return the three of us jumped into a dark-green van with Turk and started driving east on I-80 for a six-day journey across the country to Pennsylvania. With that, my life in the west came to a close without so much as a conversation to ease the many questions running through my mind. We left everything except a few random belongings that fit inside two pillow cases.

After the cross-country trip, we landed at my mom's oldest and best friend's house. Pat was a lovely lady, plump and jolly, like one might imagine a female version of Santa to be. Her husband reminded me alot of Dad and I got along well with her two children who were my age. Our friendships, however, were short-lived. After three days we hopped back into the van and drove off again, this time about an hour south.

This new destination ended with being greeted by familiar faces. While we were still in Nevada, my aunt and cousin had visited, and we had a lot of fun playing when he was there. Now the same familiar faces were there when the van doors opened up. We were greeted and welcomed into their house where we lived for the next three months. Life was a combination of a new house and a perpetual play date. We three kids were aged one year apart, and I was generally included in the games at the beginning of the time we stayed there.

For the first few weeks in this tiny new town that was as small as Reno was big, Mom was home with me in the morning before I would be off to kindergarten. Not long into our stay, however, she found work. I was sent to a sitter's house again. The boy at the end of the block was my age and in my class with me, so it made sense to go to his house before school. We became fast friends at his house, but he had other friends in our class, so I only played with him in the morning and he generally ignored me at school.

Seeds of Destruction

Part of that was because I would use the time at recess to isolate myself as I had done in our old apartment complex. I would sit alone on the merry-go-round and spin it slowly with my foot looking into the dirt for the whole break time, mostly thinking of my old friends back west, the friends for whom I never got to say good-bye. My short-lived friendship with the boy down the street ended when we moved again. While I was more prepared for this move, the severing of friendships again was not good for my social development even though our new neighborhood was full of kids my own age.

Our new house was in Meadville in a complex known at that time as Hillcrest. It was the perfect housing development in a city, set upon a hill and away from the usual bustle of the city. The main road up the complex was paved in red brick which cut each street in half so it resembled the skeleton of a fish from the sky. Our street had a full Italian family, and their son was in my class. At the end of our street were two brothers, the younger of which was in my brother's class, and down one block was a boy in my class. Later, Tony moved in on D street, two blocks down from us, with his older brother. Eventually Mick moved in one block up giving us a whole suite of new friends, and some new complications in life.

Some of these friends, like Mick, would go on to be good friends for many years, even after we all moved to different parts of the state. But mostly, like all kids, our friendships were fickle and our neighbors were often more friends of convenience rather than friends of mutual interest. This led to amazing nighttime multi-street hide-and-seek games, but also many neighborhood feuds and accusations from our constant close contact[1]. Overall, times were generally good in the neighborhood, especially after Tony moved in. He was the best childhood friend I ever had.

---

1 Proverbs 25.17

Am I Alone?

Tony first moved in around the summer after first grade, but we really first met and started talking when we were on the same walking path to school. Of course, in those days before government regulations made children sit on school buses to even transport kids a few blocks away, we all had to walk to school...uphill...both ways! Yes, we lived on the hill and the school was on another hill. Our distance was just a single mile, down Hillcrest and on the main road for a few blocks to the crossing. Then we would proceed another three blocks to a footbridge over the canyon and up the small hill to East End Elementary. Since Tony was just down the block, we got to know each other very well during the unsupervised walks to and from school each day.

We probably got along so well because we were both incessantly teased[1]. Me for my lack of social skills, and him for the thick coke-bottle glasses that magnified his eyes like a giant insect. We never talked about being teased, we just knew the pain in our respective secrets and moved on with other activities like boy scouts.

I was first introduced to the scouts when I went to one of my brother's meetings and I wanted to participate. Early on, however, I was not able to go to his meetings, and as a little second grade kid I was left home alone to play with my Micro Machines while my mom took my brother to his meetings. Once again, I was alone, and I loved it. Of course, I would stay mostly out of trouble during those years. I used that opportunity to play my copy of *Stand By Me* as background noise while I played, and I again enjoyed my solitude.

Eventually, I would join the scouts myself starting with the Tiger group, which I only recall one meeting. Once I moved up to the 'real' cub scouts, it turned out that the nearest meeting

---

1 Ecclesiastes 4:9-12

was led by Tony's dad, so my friendship with Tony grew deeper as we had meetings in his house and at his church, which was really only the second time I had been in a church to my knowledge.

Outside of scouts, I enjoyed my time playing soccer. Not that I was an athlete, in fact, I was the opposite. I was that kid who could barely run, kick, or understand how to run the field. I really was that kid who kicked the ball down the wrong side of the field. I am just glad I was such a horrible player that I wasn't able to score for the other team! Nevertheless, I enjoyed playing soccer, and I was on the team two years.

Once again, however, my friend situation was cut short. After two years in Meadville we had planned to move. So we didn't start activities so we wouldn't be pulled from them in the middle, Mom just didn't sign us up for soccer or scouts again, but we never ended up moving for another year and a half. I became socially isolated except from school, where I continued to be teased. This became a consistent pattern in my life, that every time I started to make friends, we moved.

Such was the case with kindergarten in the west; my social life started to emerge, then we moved. We stayed for three months with my cousin where I made friends with the kid down the street. But we moved again, and once we entered into a new life in a new city, and I tepidly made some friends, we moved again couple years later. The external isolation had taught me not to make friends, which may have had something to do with my later lack of social acceptance, but I'll address that later.

Mommy, Who is God?

My generation was the sad offspring of the baby boomers. Our grand parents met God on the battlefields of World War II, and dragged their future flower children off to a church service their kids didn't understand. As the boomer generation grew into adulthood, many found life's solutions in the world rather than in the church. They often gave a tip of the hat to the God their parents claimed. They had respected their parents' place of worship, but they grew up "*in* the church and not *of* the church". As they grew into adulthood and had their own kids, they often adopted the title of their parents' faith, but without a dedication to the God whose name was affixed to the church buildings. They always wanted to hand my generation the best possible life resulting in fewer of my peers being dragged to church than the previous generations.

My parents hailed from warring faiths who wanted to hook up like Romeo and Juliet. My father was raised a Catholic and my mother a Protestant of some random breed. They were united in their lack of interest in letting the church inform their life, but in those days, respectability still demanded approaching their family church for a wedding. When my dad's priest asked him why he would want to marry a "Protestant whore", that ended any desire for either of my parents to stay in the church. And they both passed their "faith", or lack there of, on to me. I subsequently went throughout life without ever thinking about any such deity as God.

Not that I *never* entered a church; it was just about as rare as a solar eclipse. Having a Catholic father, I was baptized in that tradition. It was a peace of mind to my paternal grandparents that were I to die before Confirmation, I still had an inkling of hope of visiting Saint Peter. But after the baptism ritual, I only recall stepping inside a church building once in all our time in Reno. The church I entered was one of the many day care settings I endured growing through the toddler years.

My four-year-old self recalls the old, stale toys that matched the old stale floor. The windows were beautiful stained glass—attractive from the outside. But the pews in the building were dusty and old, certainly not beautiful like the exterior suggested. The toys were too old to be exciting, and I passed my day alone with an old plastic airplane, never once knowing the purpose of such a boring building.

Eventually, we attended a church service after moving back East in the mid 1980s. The last few months of the school year included the Easter holiday at my cousin's house. My aunt and uncle were upstanding Americans in their time. This meant they were nice people who didn't commit crime, they encouraged their son in activities, and they attended exactly two church services per year.

Staying in their house over the Easter holiday meant attending one of those services with them. We walked the three blocks to the local Presbyterian church and filed in to an obviously overwhelmed church building with standing room only. I can only speculate in retrospect that the building was comfortable during the regular Sunday services.

The church service itself was an enigma. I had no idea why we were there instead of at home looking for Easter baskets. Some guy in funny black clothes would stand up and open a book while the whole group of people would repeat his words back to him. The unified tone was creepy to me; a forced obedience that didn't resonate with my rebellious mind. But it also played on my isolation. In that moment, I was totally surrounded by complete strangers, but I felt like the only one in the room who didn't know what to say.

One word was repeated throughout that church service: God. *What is God? Who is God?* The questions burned in my mind. I did what came natural to any six-year-old boy: I pulled on my mother's hand enough for her to bend down and ask what I was doing.

"Mommy, who is God?" I asked with my curious eyes catching her glance.

"The one who made everything, I guess? I don't know...don't ask again."

I didn't ask any more questions during the service. I didn't try to say the words everyone else was repeating. Easter Day, the day so celebrated in many circles, was nothing to me but a time to receive my new camouflage pajamas and a Lego set. That Sunday was the only time I had ever had a discussion about God with my mother during my childhood. Religion meant nothing in our family.

After moving into the house in Meadville, my brother made friends with our neighbor who was his age. One Sunday my brother was invited to church with them. Again, I felt left out, and I asked him questions about what the service was like. He cared for "God" as much as I did, so he told me how lucky I was that I didn't get dragged to such a boring place. We both followed our mother's faith and saw no reason to look to some deity out there beyond our reach.

Over the next two years, I considered the meaninglessness of "God" a couple times a day because our required walking path to school led us by a church building just at the bottom of the hill. The building described itself with bold letters:

Seeds of Destruction

First Church of the Nazarene

I didn't really know what 'Nazarene' was, but then sometime in my early elementary days mom and a boyfriend of her's took me to a play at the high school. The play was *The Crucifixion of Christ*, which my mother only attended because she was interested in dating. This play defined "Nazarene" for me. So I went back in my mind to The First Church of the Nazarene. It always seemed empty, and I never saw a car in the parking lot. My mind drifted back to the useless Easter service, and I asked myself why people wasted their time with such meaningless distractions as church. This place seemed as dead to me as "God" did...just beyond what was true, just beyond understanding, always out of reach. There was no "God".

Two years after we moved to Meadville, I finally found a friend in Tony. Our kindred spirits enjoyed many conversations as we passed by the dead Church of the Nazarene, or was it the church of the dead Nazarene? We talked about good things, and maybe some things not fit for children to discuss, but we never talked about God. He was more familiar with that useless deity than I. His family faithfully attended church, but he seemed to care about God as much as I did. He was another person I met who didn't take religion seriously; his parents dragged him to church in the same manner my parents were dragged in their youth.

His church sponsored our Cub Scout troop, so my evening experiences in the church building lay in the less interesting pack meetings usually occurring once a month. I always rode with Tony, and since his dad was a leader that meant arriving early to the Scout meetings and staying late, giving us time to explore the church building more than we would have been able to by attending church. It was quiet and spacious, the dark lighting made the place feel like a mausoleum. I liked to explore the dark halls of the quiet sanctuary.

Tony and I walked quietly through the hallowed halls, opening up doors, and staying mostly out of trouble. The relaxed environment gave me a peace about the church building, though attending a Sunday service removed any interest in God or church.

Being best friends with a Catholic boy meant occasionally attending the church for a service. Of the two of us, I was a little rougher around the edges. Tony and his dad seemed more 'along for the ride' than his prissy Catholic mother who was the epitome of perfection. Her meals were always perfectly on time, and she used 'dinner' for lunch, and 'supper' for dinner, totally confusing me every time she asked if I was staying for 'dinner' when Tony and I played in the morning hours. She would no doubt attend every Mass and Confession, though what she had to confess is beyond me. Looking back now, I think it was she who suggested the Saturday night sleepovers so that a wretched sinner like me would be forced into church on Sunday mornings.

I never turned down a night with a friend, so I made my way to the occasional Mass on Sunday mornings after a sleepover. I think the priests would have preferred that I stayed at home. After my first attendance, I noticed that everyone dipped their hands in that silly bowl of water and touched it to their heads. I thought it might be funny to give them something gross to rub on their faces; yes, I spit in the Holy Water! A conniving child like me knew that hocking a big ol' loogie in the bowl would be too obvious, so I got a big mouthful of spit and oozed it into my hand while approaching the bowl. My hand dipped in, dispersing my saliva through the whole chalice. I watched, laughing inside every time some poor soul would press my Holy Spit upon their forehead.

Contaminating the Holy Water was not my only way to pass time in the service. Once again, stand, sit, recite words I didn't know, stand, sit, recite words I cared not to understand. So during that long talk, I would take the bulletin and bite off little corners soaking them in more spit before launching them out of my rolled tongue into random targets in the room. I am not sure anyone ever caught on, but after that second time at church, I never attended again.

My formative years saw very little interaction with churches or God. My occasional brushes with church left me confused and bored. The few people I knew who attended church didn't seem any different from me; they just went to boring meetings once a week. I passed by the dead church, saw the boring services, and had friends who attended, but didn't take "God" seriously. It was instructive for me: "God" was dead. Useless, confusing, absent from life and meaning. Spending time on religion was a waste.

Who's My Daddy?

According to family legend, on the night I was born, my biological father was enjoying the horizontal boogie with my mom's best friend. While he ended the evening early to be in the hospital while his second son was born, my mother never gave up the anger in her heart. I didn't hear a single good thing about my father at home in all my years.

I was born into an unabiding feud; a feud that hadn't ended even into adulthood. My father was a passing stranger in my youth, not for lack of care, but because my mother couldn't carry on a civil conversation with him, and it's nearly impossible to talk to a child under twelve years of age on the telephone.

While I didn't know my biological father, I was not left without a man in the home in my earliest years. Michael lived in the motel near the trailer park where my mom and dad lived, and they became friends around the time my mom was pregnant with me. Right around then, dad moved out. Michael came over to ask about borrowing an egg, and my mom gave him the two eggs in the refrigerator. It was the last food in the house. She, being a new single and pregnant mother couldn't afford much food. Michael could afford food, but he was too busy working to stock the fridge in his motel room. This loveless act endeared my mom to Michael, so he took her out that day to stock the cupboards.

Shortly thereafter, Michael checked out of the motel and moved into the trailer. He was accepted among my mom's many friends in northwest Pennsylvania where she stayed after her own parents moved away. After a while, the job market in Erie dried up and Michael started looking for greener pastures, so he went back out west where he stayed with his dad to seek work. Once he secured employment in Reno, he sent money and train tickets. Mom took the difficult step out of her comfort zone and took her two kids for a new life out west.

The honeymoon period in Reno was every bit as glorious as a new couple expects. I had a mom, a dad, and a brother. We accumulated so many toys that exploring the bottom of our massive toy chest always yielded new discoveries. It wasn't just the things that were important. We had many good times as a young family. Our visits to Idlewild Park were the best, though the nearby lake terrified me because I would be surrounded by dozens of geese towering inches over my own head. A train museum, the circus events, and even camping at Eagle Lake seeded my early family memories.

At home every night Dad watched the news. He laid on the couch with bent legs which my imagination transformed into a spaceship for the hour just before dinner. We ate together at home or sometimes at the local A&W. At the end of the night, my brother and I would jump on a blanket which became the Choo Choo express, and we rode to bed while Dad made train noises. We were tucked into bed for the night, and another perfect day with my childhood father ended.

The real challenges happened after bedtime. Mom and Dad had an explosive relationship brought on by tight finances and personal control. Dad had a streak of jealousy and mom, a manipulative mind. They fought in the evenings after the quiet day and their screams pierced the silence in our bedroom. Holes appeared in the walls overnight and ashtrays shattered against furniture. While we had fun times with Dad, my mom contended with a tyrant.

Lack of commitment fueled Mom's conflict. "Marry me, or I'll leave you," she threatened. Michael called the bluff, so they hopped in the car and drove to Carson City. The sign on Main Street pointed the way with the helpful direction, 'Marriage Licenses 6 Blocks This Way'. After a fight and a threat, they eloped, with a hired witness at a 'Create Your Dreams' chapel in Nevada. My brother and I slept through the ceremony in the back of Michael's black Datsun, passing out in matching black suits, white shirts, and red ties like a pair of tiny Mormons.

Marriage and commitment is supposed to make everything right with the world, well, at least that is the dream sold us like a blue-light special. In reality, marriage is more like a condenser. For a couple deeply in love, the marriage strengthens the bonds of friendship, but for people in conflict, the condenser purifies the anger, increasing the odds of exploding into a fight.

Fights got worse and mom looked for ways to escape. She occasionally came home unexpectedly, grabbed us kids with a few belongings before running off with guys she met at work. On one such occasion we moved into a desert shack outside of Reno. While playing, we were cornered by a rattlesnake. Yelling for help summoned this strange man my mom brought with us. He killed the snake, but I was not comforted in that place. By the end of weekend, Michael showed up and brought us home. There were at least two times we ran off with other guys, but we always ended up back at home, and that is where I was happiest.

The day we finally left Reno started like any other day. We got up after mom and dad left for work. My brother and I watched *Kids Corporation* and *Transformers*, the end of which signified when we needed to leave the house. My brother to the bus stop, and me to the babysitter's house just outside the stairs leading up to our second story apartment door. I walked our complex alone for the last time, though I didn't know it would be my last. The day was as normal as could be as I went off to my afternoon kindergarten class. My brother and I got off the bus and walked through our construction site looking at the shiny black rocks. We made our way to check in with the babysitter, but Mom opened the door, and we made a hasty escape from Reno with Turk.

After a couple days on the road I thought Michael might find us and bring us home like he always did, but mom said that wasn't going to happen. I started to look to Turk to take his place. He was a man, sounded about the same, behaved about the same, so I gave him a chance. He was there when we first landed at Pat's house, and still there when we left for our aunt and uncle's house. I thought for sure he was the new 'dad', until mom told me he was leaving. So three days after we landed at my cousins, he gave me a final ride to school, then I never saw Turk again.

Over the next several months, mom secretly planned to move us to our own place. She spent her time seeking a new career since Pennsylvania had a notable lack of keno runners. She didn't meet any new boyfriends during that transitional period, but one day in the summer after we moved to Meadville, we were going up to Pat's house.

On the way, Mom said we were going to McDonald's in the Millcreek Mall. Two boys had no objection to such a splendid proposal. Once there, Mom introduced us to a man she called 'Dad'. This was a little confusing for me because I knew Dad, and this guy wasn't him. We talked to this perfect stranger for a while. He gave us a parting gift of a remote control car that was probably better suited for older kids. We were never permitted to play with the car which resided in a cupboard above the refrigerator. Maybe it was just a symbol of That Man.

Later in the summer we went and stayed with Strange Dad for a weekend. We weren't comfortable at his house. It was like visiting a total stranger overnight. The rules were not understood and the boundaries went untested. On top of the strangeness of being at his house, it was also the most boring place to be in the universe. At least Grandma's house had a few old toys and a big backyard, but Strange Dad didn't have anything. We slept on the hard floor in sleeping bags. He didn't have a television, couch, chairs, toys—nothing but a pool table, a bistro table nestled in the corner of the kitchen, and a small bed in his bedroom. We felt like we visited an empty storehouse in a way.

A couple years later we visited Strange Dad again, but this time we stayed at his work instead of his house. It was immediately apparent that he spent a lot more time in the old factory which now was an office for the startup tool-and-die company he was creating. The old building was right next to the boat docks; a dream location for Strange Dad who always wanted to live on a boat. The factory building was large and mostly empty, but here he had a television and a giant queen sized mattress where we were able to sleep more comfortably. He also had exercise equipment, but nothing else a kid would like.

What he did have was fishing equipment. An avid fisherman would probably not be excited to hook a hotdog on the end of the hook and dip it into Lake Erie for a hot second before snagging a useless bluegill, but to me, it was the most fun I ever had. When engaging an activity like 'fishing', Strange Dad was curiously fun. I'm sure in retrospect he was getting annoyed at the number of bluegill he had to throw back, but it gave me an exciting first fishing expedition.

Of the three times we visited Strange Dad in our elementary school years, one was full of boredom in his empty house, one was near the boat dock with a little excitement, but our last trip was actually on his boat. Somewhere in that period of time, he fulfilled the first steps of his dreams and bought a little house boat that was docked right at his office. My brother and I shared the stern room of the boat, a little space with two beds much more comfortable than the floor at his house. During that trip we boated out into the middle of lake, did more fishing from the boat, swam in the deep part of the lake, and even attended a party on a yacht. Also, on that trip, I got sick, which may have been the flu going around or it may have been sea-sickness. I just remember mom being mad at him for 'getting me sick' and it was quite a while before I visited Strange Dad again.

A few months into the new school year right after we moved to Meadville, I was in my first grade classroom when there was a knock on the door. Mrs. Stanton opened the door and in walked Mom!

"I have a surprise for you," she said, handing the teacher a note to get me out of class for the rest of the day.

I was escorted from the room. My brother and I were instructed to close our eyes. To be sure we didn't peek, Mom covered our eyes with her hands and walked us down one echoing, empty hall after another. We turned left, then mom said to open our eyes. Michael sat on the bench just outside the office.

"Dad!" we both shrieked, running into his embrace.

Dad came home. The real one, and not the strange one. With Dad's arrival, our toy budget blossomed again and things looked like they would be perfect forever more. We were back to a happy, two parent home. Dad also brought with him the return of occasional surprises like that night they told us to get our blanket and pillow because we were going to go to a drive-in movie. We drove and drove; much longer than it usually took us to get to a movie theater. Dad just said to go to sleep, and they would wake me up when we got there. I fell asleep for the night and woke up in a strange room, but Mom and Dad were there, so all was perfect with the world.

We left the hotel room and walked a bit to a giant waterfall. In the night, they drove us to see Niagara Falls. We looked around the falls, the attractions, and museums. It was a good day, a hearkening to the old days of fun family vacations.

We also took a trip to the now abandoned Geauga Lake. The trip combined the best of family life: stopping at a toy store, a camp site right on the lake by the amusement park, and a full day at the amusement park. This was the final confirmation that the good old days would last forever.

But all wasn't right with the world. The return of Dad also brought the return of the late night arguments, only worse. Every time a drunkard 'quits' drinking, the next relapse results in greater drunkenness, and when an angry couple gets back together, the fights intensify. Their fights became more fierce and the noises pierced the sanctuary of our room into the late evenings. Mom and Dad finally collected their cool enough to make a joint decision to divorce, and just to make sure it would stick, Michael planed to move back to the west coast without us.

It was a school day when I found out Dad was leaving. They pulled me out of school early that day and we drove up the hill in Mom's old Chevy Nova to send a bunch of boxes out west by bus. We finally stopped at Dairy Queen in Meadville where I ordered the favorite Blizzard of my young life: chocolate ice cream with M&Ms.

While sitting in the booth, sun shining on me through the annex of curved glass, they finally told me that Dad was leaving and wouldn't be coming home. I shed many tears in between the Blizzard bites, bouncing between the joy of ice cream and the sadness of Dad moving away. We finished our ice cream, me in tears, and headed for the two cars in the parking lot. I wanted to ride home with Dad, but that wasn't possible. From my seat in the back of the Nova, I watched as his green Mustang took the right hand turn up the hill. We exited to the left, back toward town. I turned to look out the window, watching for any sign of his car following us, but it was not. Dad never came home again.

Dad leaving sent my brother and I down some deep spirals. He found comfort in friends while I walked the streets in our complex alone. I enjoyed the isolation and quiet, but the solitude didn't do any favors to my mannerisms. I grew more isolated and that led to some delinquencies. But as much as we kids were struggling, Mom struggled all the more. She longed for the perfect husband and father; someone who, like her own dad, would raise the kids, support her, and help with the bills. She kept looking for Prince Charming in all the weirdest places (judging by the characters she would date).

The shortest lived relationship was that guy who took us to the Jesus play. I am not sure if Mom knew what kind of play it was, or if she just didn't care. Maybe she didn't know the guy she went with was religious. I have no recollections of him, and I am pretty sure that was the last time Mom saw him, unless that was also the same unmemorable guy who bought our Nova when we picked up a rusty old station wagon.

Who's My Daddy?

One prime example of the pure-blood Pennsylvania Redneck she picked up was named – I kid you not – Bonecutter! She found him working the gas station / auto repair store down the road from Hillcrest. He invited us out to his backwoods paradise one evening for a good ol' fashion hoedown. His house was contained on a large parcel of property in a little pine forest. It was littered with multiple broken down cars in the driveway. I felt like I was visiting Neverland.

He had some kids who were close to our age, but they were more prepared for life than my brother and me. Despite their young age, they were out cutting firewood, and doing so with safety in mind. Always sure of where everyone was, and being careful with their handling, they cut firewood with precision. I wanted a swing of that ax, so they handed it to me, but it was very apparent I had never handled such a weapon before, and being surrounded by half-a-dozen kids and no adults is not the place to learn how to handle an ax. They quickly separated me from my instrument of death and talked about safety once again. We had a meal, met some people, but after that outing we never saw Bonecutter again.

Soon after that dinner party, we went to a classic Redneck Barbecue. It was not all that different than the party at Bonecutter's house, and to this day I am convinced the festivities were held in a junkyard. There were several broken down old cars in various stages of decay. A few large coolers overflowed with various cans near a table of chips in between two fires, one of which was populated mostly by kids while the other, adults. The kids popped open Faygo colas while the adults busted open beer after beer. I was like a fish out of water in such a place. Being unable to relate to the rest of the little hicklets, I just sat by the fire bidding my time until we left. I didn't know it at the time, but that was the first "family audition" with William.

37

Seeds of Destruction

William was another Pennsylvania Hick. He was a van driver for the county ambulance service, and my mother was often accompanying residents of the nursing home on various outings. William asked her out on a date, and the story goes that she told him on that first dinner that, "It was a good thing my last husband left, I was going to poison him." Of course, William still wanted a woman, but being nervous, he never let her cook for him during their long courtship.

This man was quite different from Michael. While the latter was interested in parental responsibility, William seemed to hate kids...or maybe that was just people. He had the personality of a neanderthal, grunting more than communicating, and avoiding contact with people as much as possible, while at least outside of work. He didn't want anything to do with kids, and while they dated for the rest of our time in Meadville, he only came over to our house once when we were moving out. That was just to patch the holes and fix severed phone cords left behind by Michael's bouts of rage. In addition, we only visited his house twice. He tolerated us kids as much as he could, only communicating with us when avoiding the nagging Mom gave him about "teaching her boys" life lessons.

When I look back now to my early life, I had a real father I never knew, a father I loved whom I could not have, various boyfriends I never knew, and one long term boyfriend who didn't like kids. So who is dad, again?

Can I Have That?

I love the show, *Hoarders;* It isn't because I like to see people turn their houses into rat-infested death traps, nor do I like to see their suffering. I like the show because there is a potential hoarder inside all of us. Having watched enough episodes, it is clear that the show is not about parading people's ugly hoards in front of the world for ridicule, but rather, it is about helping those poor souls to overcome the deeper issues in their lives which has led to such a hoard in the first place. Of course, the root issue behind most hoarding is loss.

People who suffer loss can be pushed to the extreme of collecting anything. Even garbage could be clung to with such a voracity so as to provide comfort. Even the cleanest, most organized adult can turn into a filthy hoarder given enough loss in their life. Some loss is the natural course of life; people do die. Spouses who are full of life can leave behind a loved one, and those left behind spend decades in mourning, never really emotionally overcoming the loss in their family. Other losses can be a tragedy, like an accident, or a fire as my own mother experienced in her childhood. Others, like myself, it could be traumatic life experiences, as some would even say, the loss of childhood itself.

I have suffered a lot of loss in my early years. My first five years of life were pretty good. Mom and Dad bought us a lot of toys; maybe even too many. We had accumulated enough toys to necessitate a custom-built toy box to house our growing pile of play things.

This box was big enough for both me and my brother to fit into perfectly as little children. In fact, I might even fit into it today. Measuring four feet long and two feet wide is big, but a height of three-and-a-half feet tall made it difficult to even access for such a young kid. That massive box took up the corner in our bedroom, and when our room was clean, that box was about three quarters full. We enjoyed our toys, whether they be the legacy Spiderman and Hulk toys of our pre-memory days, or else the new Hotwheels race track and bedtime Carebear that I received for Christmas scarce weeks before we left everything behind, including my little red bicycle with training wheels.

My toys were not the only loss in my life. I loved Dad; I loved pretending his folded legs were my spaceship as he lay on the couch watching the evening news. I loved the rafting trip down the river and the times enjoying a root beer float at the local A&W. Our trips to the local pizza shop were things of memories. I just loved a man in my life, even if it was not the best relationship possible. I didn't know of dysfunction, but really, I didn't care to look for it. Our family was just as normal as everybody else: Two working parents, piles of toys, and trips to Eagle Lake. I didn't even know anything was wrong when Dad was left behind.

Five, going on six, is an age when we start becoming aware of all the other people around us. I enjoyed my time in kindergarten. I started the beginning steps of making friends with the kids in the class. I remember the twins best of all. Sally was my first 'girlfriend.' She even kissed my cheek on the bus when we were on the way back to school after walking though the Christmas Tree display in town. Her and Susie were my best friends in class, and many other kids my own age started to blossom in my growing social circle, though again, one day, they were all left behind.

Can I Have That?

After our cross-country trip, we started settling down at my cousins house. We went from a two parent home in Reno, to a three parent home in the east. I picked up another playmate in my cousin. It wasn't all a good adjustment, as I didn't recall making any new friends in my new class, but I met the neighbor boy who was my age. All these new connections were short-lived, however, because right at the end of the school year we moved again, this time to a new city.

Our move to Meadville resulted in more loss. Our new adjusted home of three parents was reduced to one hard-working mother and two boys who both hurt inside their heart. While mom succeeded at providing food and shelter, the cost included working third shift at a local nursing home and sleeping the day away. There was balance in being awake in the evenings to cook us dinner and watch a few television programs before heading off to another shift. Our first summer was lonely. Mom slept all day and my brother found a few kids in the new neighborhood his age, so he took it upon himself to regularly ditch his annoying little brother.

I was left to wander the streets in our complex alone, brooding in my memories of times gone by and good toys left behind– not once, but twice. So one cool, early morning I walked down the street with my head down as usual. I thought of my past wandering in the Reno apartments. Something caught the corner of my eye: a little car just on the edge of a random yard. Micro Machines were the new rage; the toys I coveted ever since seeing them on television. I looked around to the left and to the right. Seeing no motion in either direction I causally bent down and feigned messing with my shoe as my fingers glided over the precious plastic and steel. My fingers circled around the baby car and I palmed it, again glancing around to make sure no one was watching me. I picked up my pace, walking faster to the edge of the street catching the little path up to the two water towers on the edge of the woods. I finally stopped and looked down at the little car, admiring the detail. This was the first thing I ever stole. My thought process at the time knew it was wrong to take it[1], hence my caution and quickened steps, but I wanted it for my own. My reduced toy budget saddened me, and I tried to grasp tightly for anything I could hold, even if I had to steal it.

Of course, having no other Micro Machines, and knowing inside myself that it was wrong to steal, I now clutched a toy I couldn't play with openly. The dilemma was mostly OK since I spent more time alone than with family, but the acquisition started a secret collection of trinkets. My collection was that one little thing I knew about which no one else did. If they didn't know about it, they couldn't take it. This collection was one thing I reasoned that I could not lose[2]. Starting with my first grand-theft-micro-auto, a new collection blossomed. Mostly, the possessions were acquired innocently by finding them in exploration.

One item in my collection was a coveted little tin container with a sliding lid. I found this while exploring the church after a Cub Scout meeting. I opened it and closed it. I admired the scent of the pink substance inside it, but I didn't know it was lip gloss, or even what such a thing would be for, but the container pleased me. I slipped this quickly into my pocket and never told anyone about it. Once we were home that night, it found its way into my secret bag of private possessions that no one could take from me.

Some of my belongings were more terrifying, such as a box of 0.38 caliber bullets. Sometime in the summer after dad had left, Mom and I went hiking with a guy she dated for a period of

---

1 Jeremiah 31·33
2 Matthew 10·39

Can I Have That?

time. He was a woodsy man who wanted to show her a hiking trail, so while my brother spent time with friends, I went along for a hike with Mom and the new guy. Along the trail I stopped to pee. I looked down on the ground by the freshly watered tree to see a red and white box. Curious type that I was, I picked it up. I expected an empty box, but it was heavy. I slid the box open and a bullet fell out. I was startled. I picked up the fresh round and admired it for a moment before cramming it back into the box. I slipped the whole payload back into my little pocket. To this day I have no idea how they didn't find out I was toting around a box of bullets all day. The box was my prize possession in my secret little cache.

Aside from the shiny things I found on the ground outside, I started becoming an accomplished kleptomaniac. Some thieves steal for material or financial gain, but I stole to hold onto a little piece of this fleeting world. So I picked up a salamander fishing lure from a friends garage under his nose while we explored in there. I'm not sure such a thing would have been noticed missing, but I loved my new pilfered rubber creature. I also picked up a knife that lay on the table at William's house when we stopped there to pee on the way home from Pat's house one day. When confronted on that one, they believed my spectacular lie, so the knife stayed hidden away in the collection.

My largest and most impressive hide was when we visited the construction site for our new house that was being built. While looking around, I saw a box of copper pipe joints. I helped myself to a collection of about six shiny pieces and hid them nicely in my jacket, trying not to clang them together on the inside pocket. The most impressive part about this find was how well I hid them for the rest of the night. We went to McDonald's on the way home, so I feigned being cold to keep my jacket on so copper pipe joints wouldn't rain down on the hard bench exposing my crime. I made it home without anyone knowing I totted around several shiny copper trinkets.

Having learned to be a thief and a liar to hoard my precious belongs, those skills started bleeding into delinquency[1]. I already knew what I was doing was wrong, so what is a little more excitement? I loved the movie *Stand By Me*, which I watched every Tuesday when my brother attended his scout meeting. The kids on that movie became my role models[2]. The sneakiness, the cussing, and of course, the smoking taught me how to be cool, so I looked for the opportunity to get some smokes.

At the end of our street their resided a descendant from the brave William Mead who founded our city. This present specimen, however, was not the shining example of his ancestors. He grew into adulthood and still lived with his mom. He never accomplished more than sitting on the front porch smoking half a cigarette before tossing it into the bushes. I got up early in the morning to gather the half-consumed smokes, slipping them into my pocket for being cool later. I kept them hidden until I could snag a lighter, which didn't take long since our babysitter smoked. I grabbed her lighter and sneaked a few new cigarettes from her stash before disappearing into the woods to start my new bad habit right there in the summer between my first and second grades.

My solitude became the time to engage in behavior that wore down my conscience[3], but the more we wear down our inner voice, the easier it becomes to take our misbehavior to the next level. After Dad left, we visited grandma for a week. She was a chain smoker and never low on packs of Paul Mall. While exploring her house, stealing some time away from my brother,

---
[1] James 1·14-15
[2] 1 Corinthians 15·33
[3] Isaiah 6·10

Can I Have That?

I was also stealing a full pack of smokes from a carton left unattended. I slipped them into my bag and looked at them often, not wanting to open the pack up until making it home, but once there, I wanted to share my habit with my new friend, Tony[4]. I rolled my cigarette pack up in my sleeve like Chris Chambers[5], and we walked through the woods; I walked taller than I ever had before. I was, after all, a cool kid with a pack of smokes. The two of us walked through our woods until we reached Octopus Tree: a big white oak on the edge of the forested part of the trail in the woods. We sat on the rock just above the little stream and lit up our smokes to be cool little second graders.

In all this, I learned to steal to get what I wanted. Asking was hard, taking was easy. I learned to build up my little collection to hold onto the parts of the world, because the rest of my life spun out of control. Stealing became my way of controlling something, as wrong and vain as it may have been.

---

4 Proverbs 1:10
5 Chris Chambers was the leader of the group of kids in *Stand By Me*.

Can You Keep a Secret?

Generations of overly religious parents have echoed the old adage, "Idle time is the Devil's plaything." Such a phrase has reeked havoc on the summer vacations of teenage sons and daughters, forcing them to find a dreaded summer job. The exact origin of this expression is not known, but an old church saint said something like it, in Latin, of course. The phrase was eventually translated into old, dead English by the romantic poet Geoffrey Chaucer. The translation carries the same connotations: keep yourself busy, or a red, pitchfork wielding devil will show up to make you do bad things. In hindsight, I completely agree with the sentiment. If our society allowed kids to find jobs earlier, many tragedies of conscience may be avoided. In fact, a summer job for a random teenager may have prevented a young woman from using her idle time with me when I was five years old.

I often played with the girl from across the way during the summer break between preschool and kindergarten. She was my babysitter's daughter, so we had a lot of opportunity to play together, and we often played in the safe walkways between our parallel apartment buildings. One day, a teenage girl started talking to us, and after earning our trust, said she had something to show me. The little girl guarded the steps leading up the dark corridor that led to a landing where my apartment door was situated. The single overhead light provided just enough illumination for the teenager's "something" to be shown. She slid her pants down, pointing to the hairy mess that lay perpendicular to my face. She showed me where to put my hands, and where to move them, and how to move them around. This exploration was strangely fun, and completely gross, all wrapped up in a single horrible secret. Exploration occurred more than once and led to a variety of explorations of me, her, and us together.

Sensing the secrecy of the matter but looking to explore all the more, the sitter's daughter became my new expedition grounds. We were caught playing "doctor" a few times, but the worst incident was a day my brother and I were at the babysitter's house. The girl tried to sit down on my brother, who told her to stop, so I said she can sit on me! Before long, both our pants were down, and we were trying to emulate the things the teenager did to me in the upper corridor. Her mom walked in, and we were busted. Needless to say, that was the last time I was ever in her bedroom!

Playing "doctor" spread to a few neighborhood acquaintances in my five-year-old life. I also played it once with a neighbor boy. I was the youngest kid in the room during a sleepover, so I was "selected" to be the doctor, and us three boys stayed up all night exploring and being explored. This was the last time the "doctor" was on call in the West, and that may have ended this childhood nonsense if it were not for the events that happened a couple years later.

My brother met the kids down the block shortly after we moved to Meadville. Like me and my brother, they were also two years apart in age, but the younger one, was in my brother's class in school. We often went to their house during the long summer hours. On one such hot day after second grade we were at their house when one of the boys said he found his dad's "movies". We liked movies, so he popped in a VHS tape, but this was no *Snow White and the Seven Dwarfs*! Our wide eyes watched a row of naked men being serviced by a row of naked ladies to the bitter end. Such a film resurrected memories of the teenager in Reno, and I knew this movie was another secret that demanded to be kept.

My brother's classmate added to the secrets after viewing this movie. Wanting to emulate what he saw on that old VHS tape, he invited me over because I was the youngest kid in the neighborhood. He moved beyond exploring and had me repeat the actions he saw on the tape. I hated the events and being used, but I loved the attention I was getting.

The secret burned inside me. Such secrets long to escape, but never to the people who should hear them; never to those who can make the world right. So one day, my classmate from a few streets down the hill was in my room playing some innocent Transformers scene from the latest episode when I finally spoke up.

"Can you keep a secret?" I asked.

"What is it?" He inquired.

"Can you keep one?"

"Yes, what is it?"

I unfolded my secrets about the kid at the end of the block and the video we watched, then I asked if he wanted to try it. So we explored that day, and also a few other times at the end of the summer into the start of the next school year. But as fate would have it, we wanted to let another classmate in on the secret. We invited him up to my room when my mom was out one day. This boy had good parents who taught him how to lie at just the right times and that there are secrets better exposed. He told our secret to his parents, who blabbed to the school, and I was sent to the guidance counselor's office the following Monday. I lied to him about the extent of the secret, only admitting to the surface of what he already knew. The secret had to be kept.

I felt like I dodged a bullet for the rest of the school day, but when I walked in the door that afternoon, Mom was awake, which was unusual. She wanted to talk. Obviously, the guidance counselor had called home to report the situation. I can only imagine how that phone call went, but the consummation was my bad deeds with the neighbor boys. They only knew the surface of the crime. The secret had to be kept, but Mom tried to get more out of me. Master manipulator she was, she lied to attempt to coerce a confession, but no confession could be extracted. We were in a stalemate, two fortified wills which wouldn't be broken. Finally, plugging one ear and holding the other close, she whispered,

"Tell me about what you did, I will never, ever tell anyone."

She received only the surface confession she already had from the counselor. The secret had to be kept. I was let off to play, and we never discussed the topic again. I dodged another bullet and went out to play. But after returning home for dinner, I walked into the dinning room. Michael instantly grabbed me with a voracity usually reserved for late night fights with Mom. His loud screams terrified me to my core; I wasn't able to discern what he said. I also know that my brother was informed of the matter, and for telling my secret, I knew I couldn't trust my mother, who lied about not telling anyone my secret. At least my brother was there to stop his friend one night when he was over and wanted to try those things again.

Elementary age kids are not as ignorant of sex as their parents often think. That was even true before the Information Age. Kids often lack the specific words and actions, but the general concepts and feelings involved in sex spread through elementary schools like a pandemic. I made one accidental connection to this world while playing in the park. Betting myself I could reach the top of the pole elevating the basketball hoop, I shimmied up the pole only to find part way up that things down there felt tingly and good. I climbed that pole in the park many times after discovering this, but the connection between those feelings and sex was made on one of the walks to school with Tony. During the course of the conversation, I mentioned the video we watched. Wanting to know more about those feelings, we tried to emulate the actions of that video on several occasions. It was our little secret again, and one that we swore to ourselves, so no one else could ever find out.

We tried those things in my bedroom when no one was home, and we even did them often in the woods on the rock at Octopus Tree in between our cigarettes. It was our secret to keep, and we felt like a 'club' so we called ourselves "The Tarantulas" and drew the name and a crudely drawn spider on each other's arm like the gang in *Stand By Me*. Two outcasts who sought to be accepted sought comfort in each other. We found our bad influences in people and videos[1]. What started with a random teenager thousands of miles away, a video kept not hidden enough by a father on the block, no parental guidance, and way too much idle time, I learned about sexuality when I was way too young.

---

1 For a deeper dive in the impact media and entertain has on us, check out my book *I AM not amused*.

Flowing Times

September 3, 2000

A boy first learns to walk,
Followed by the ability to talk
"Go, have fun, make friends"
But shortly after, it fell to ends
Without good bye, we jumped in back,
Very little, we did pack
Six days gone, another three,
A big green house with a climbing tree
Stayed for a while, more friends came,
We left again. Am I to blame?
I hesitate to learn new geography,
For at any given moment we may flee.
Nice white house with a large green lawn,
Red shutters and the sunlight of dawn
Why did we go? Where is Dad?
Haven't seen him in a while. I'm sad
Mom goes off to work tonight,
Leaving me only a small dim light.
Brother and me alone again,
Was it like this way back then?
I hear nothing below,
Not even a painful blow.
Is it good he is gone?
Or does he truly belong?
It seems so long I've been here,
I didn't get any friends near.
I was afraid of leaving again,
Just like way back then.
Comfort finally starts setting in,
I think for once I may grin.
Happy days are here to stay,
I've finally found a good day.

Can You Keep a Secret?

Happy times in the woods,
Two of us stood.
I found a friend to share myself,
He in turn offered himself
Others come with hope of lasting,
And I can finally rest my passing.
Many adventures we did share,
In weather cold, hot, and fair.
For some of us, the woods did call,
And others, the pool was all.
We built forts including fire,
Then we rest our constant tire.
All around, we learned our land,
And had fun there hand for hand.
The top of the hill there were some vines,
Which became our playground all the time.
Swinging from tree to tree,
It was fun to be so free.
But one day that would end,
"Dear sons, we're moving again."
So again all was gone away,
My safety gone in just a day.
I had nothing but a brother,
And of course a mother.
No father, no friends,
No where to go in the end.
A new place, a new beginning,
For a ten year old to try again.
Different culture, different land,
It felt like no one would hold my hand.
Night after night, I cried some tears,
Not even they could breech the fears.
I tried hard not to cry,
But I tried even harder not to die.
New lands to explore,
But no motivation any more.
Again I had to start again,

Seeds of Destruction

Just like way back then.
More people thought it fun,
To make me just feel shunned.
This seemed to anger me,
So they continued to tease me.
The harder I tried to be like them,
The more they pushed me from them.
I bowed to their sports,
But I just became a dork.
I tried to fit in,
They just kicked my shin.
I ran home and cried again,
I just wanted to be let in.
I finally just gave up,
I couldn't catch, throw, or jump.
This continued on and on,
But one day it started to be gone.
I found a friend and we had fun,
Exploring was good fun.
We learned anew,
From many clues.
We had fun in several places,
Just as in life's little mazes.
I would ride over in the morning,
Fun would be 'til twilight dawning.
Fun continued only for a short,
His own parents cut it short.
Moving him away,
From fun every day.
It hurt me too, but I still had one,
So on continued the fun.
Mischief set in,
Allowing "bad" stuff in.
We learned the bombs, blew them up,
Which made the summer seem up.
And all was going great again,
Then history wrinkled again.

One Wicked Sapling

*Do not enter the path of the wicked
And do not proceed in the way of evil men.*
Proverbs 4:14

Is There a Friend for Me?

About the time I was being a determinant to Tony's behavior, Mom decided we needed to move so the bad influences in the city wouldn't negatively impact our lives. (Just a hint for like-minded parents: the influences are everywhere. Prepare, don't run!) She had saved up enough money for a down payment and conscripted a contractor to build a house in a new town. Our plans to move were delayed several times, and my mother didn't want to start activities we could not finish, so she didn't sign me up for soccer or scouts after second grade. Our unsupervised time compounded our mischievousness. But alas, the time had come, and on the unlucky day of Friday the Thirteenth, we moved from our old rented house in the city to a brand-new house in the suburbs...deep into the suburbs.

The mean Meadville kids morphed into new little Edinboro devils who were down-right cruel. The little town of 7000 residents lived in the shadow of a University that doubled the population during the school year, but generally, campus life didn't bleed into the little main street of family owned businesses like larger university towns. Edinboro, however, didn't have an identity apart from the high school sports teams.

The principal walked me down the hallways of Edinboro Elementary talking about how much I will like the new teacher. With a knock of the door, the beautiful young lady just out of college smiled and pointed to a desk at the end of a row of kids donning smiling faces.

This is much better than Meadville, I had thought to myself. Then one of the boys whispered to me. I expected a "Hi" or "I'm Ricky", but I was instead asked the fateful question: "Do you play football?"

I traveled back in my mind to a horrible birthday party in first grade where all the kids knew what football was and how to play it. That fated party would be the last time I was invited to anyone's birthday outside immediate family and Tony. I whispered back, "No."

That was it. I was placed instantly in the *out* crowd by the wealthy progeny of the washed-out sports stars of the last generation. I found myself in a town devoid of identity outside the football team. Me, a sports ignoramus, never stood a chance with the popular kids!

From day one recess was a nightmare. Give me essays and spelling tests; math problems and reading was more pleasurable than being either the new kid or the outcast, of which I was both wrapped up in one tormentable package. At first, they gave me a chance, but I was doomed the moment I threw the football like a girl (and not the tom-boy girl of our class). They tested my skills as a receiver instead, but they found paraplegics who made a better receiver than me. I wasn't ever invited to play again. I was cast out with the other male reject of the class, who was even too extreme for me.

I tried to fit in. I saw the kids liked football cards, so I spent my allowance to buy cards hoping they would accept me into the group. They stole my cards instead. For my birthday just after moving to this god-forsaken town, I wasted a present on a football, but they just took it from me and played a non-consensual game of *pouting, angry monkey* in the middle. I was good for their laughs, but each laugh they uttered turned into pent-up tears for me.

It was very clear to Mom that I wasn't making friends, so she signed me up for an after school play group in the school gymnasium. It was supposed to be used to socialize the kids, but all it accomplished was greater ostracization. I was now incubated with the same kids who tormented me all day, but with less structure and supervision. Didn't I suffer enough?

One evening I went for a bike ride around the block with Mom. In the wealthier part of the subdivision, a dozen or so kids were all collected in a backyard playing more football. Mom, thinking it would be good, told me to ask if I can join them. They stopped their huddle when they saw me, but they didn't ask me to play, nor did I want to ask. It was evening and I had already endured my daily torture. Please, no more.

As the school year passed by and bled into summer, I mostly hung around with my brother who was given instructions to take me with him anywhere he went. We often played with the neighbor kid, Nathan, three years my junior. We didn't specifically like him, but he was the only other kid in the neighborhood who didn't still wear diapers. He was the classic fair-weather friend, and even his parents didn't care for us much. They suspected that we treated our little friend's house as a five-finger discount store. We played in Nathan's overstocked basement of toys and always walked out with something in our pocket. At some point his parents caught onto our delinquency, but being gracious, they banned us from the house rather than confronting us about it[1].

The summer ended and I started middle school. Our middle school combined our little town with the hicks from the northern country between us and Erie. The McKean hicks were much nicer kids, not as prone to tease, nor were they as obsessed with football. More kids made recess better when the

---

1 Proverbs 15:1

jocks were diluted down. The football game seemed smaller, but there were other kids I could play with who were more like me. Though all the McKean kids were kept in one group and the Edinboro kids in the other group in our first year of middle school, to "better adjust us", they said.

In my case, adjustment wasn't the problem. I wrestled with the barrage of teasing, which didn't only come from the students. I had a teacher for half the day that also found pleasure in teasing me. She found that if she threw the occasional insult my way, it would make the other kids laugh. This, of course, empowered them to tease me all the more. I told Mom about the teasing from the teacher and mom asked about it. The teacher just said she "liked me a lot." Then she told me I need a better sense of humor. It hurt. Day in and day out, my fifth grade year fueled nightmares for any middle school boy. I was insulted from the students and teachers, from mom and my brother. "Get a sense of humor" "Learn to take a joke" "Ignore it" voiced the advice of fools!

More anxiety mounted as our school made a three-day class outing. A local camp gave the school a huge discount to bring in the fifth grade kids every year. Of course we went in our usual school groups, so I was sent to camp in fifth grade for three days with the kids who gave every appearance of hating me.

The activities and staff at the camp were nice, but I was in constant dread of my classmates. They had managed to find every way possible to tease me, whether it was my lack of athletic behavior, or the way I would dress myself in the morning (once, my mom even yelled at me, in front of my friends, that I dressed like a f---ing Polack), or if I passed gas. This was disconcerting to me because I had the habit of what psychologists call 'headbanging' where I hit my head repeatedly against the pillow at night, often making noise. My mother gave me the admonishing, 'don't do that' as if I actually had control over a habit born from her arguments with Michael! I lived in terror for three days, becoming robotic; conscious of every movement I made.

Even with my care they granted me a new nickname. The bathrooms were communal, and I was already uncomfortable around these kids, so I didn't want to strip in front of them to take a communal shower, particularly with the way other kids had treated me in Meadville. I didn't shower on the first two days, so I was named "Stinky" on that camping trip. I couldn't wait to go home. I was miserable, and it wasn't homesickness!

I survived the fifth grade, and we coasted through the summer with a new neighborhood frienemy (a kid who was sometimes a friend and sometimes an enemy). He moved onto the block that summer and we mostly shared an interest in Nintendo and GI Joe. While we loved Transformers in our previous life, we switched to GI Joe as a sign of the new "us" in the new neighborhood, so we often played at his house because his mom was over-protective. He only came to our house when his older half brother visited over the weekends.

After our mostly peaceful summer, it was time for school to start again. Sixth grade treated me better since the school integrated our group. I had friends from McKean in class scattered among the kids who incessantly teased me to no end. The teachers were also all nice and without teasing, so by the end of the school year, I actually had a few kids I comfortably called friends.

Jake was my best friend for the latter half of middle school. He had moved to town in the middle of the school year in sixth grade. On his first day in school he tried to take my friend's hat, though it was all in clean fun. Me, being clueless to playful teasing, tried to come to the aid and get the hat back. I pulled back as hard as I could and hit Jake square in the face. He laughed. My strongest punch would fail to phase a toddler, for I was the king of ninety-pound weaklings.

Recess ended and I licked my wounded pride. We filed into Mr. White's classroom for sixth period. The teacher introduced Jake as the new student, and class began. On this day, we watched a film, and Mr. White, one of our best teachers, allowed us to sit next to friends during movies. Lacking any of those in this class, I decided to sit with an enemy instead. I moved to Jake's area and apologized for hitting him, but he said it was funny. From that day on, we were best of friends.

Jake lived in town unlike my other friends. While his house was way on the other end of town, we were easily able to meet up at the mall located halfway between our houses. As the school year turned into summer, we had some early adventures, but I was grounded for a week right at the beginning of the school year. Jake rode his bike across town when I told him I was grounded and to come back next week. Of course, as soon as we were let off being grounded, we were grounded again for another month. He came back and I gave him the news.

As mischievous kids, he left for a few minutes, and then we met up at my window to talk while Mom slept in the other room. My mind crafted a devious plan: I was given a task (call it work release?) to walk to the local Giant Eagle to buy hamburger meat. Since I already accomplished that task early, I hid the meat and we walked out of sight of the house to sneak an hour of time with my best friend.

Robert was another other friend from school who lived in McKean, so I rarely saw him outside of school. Near the end of the summer, he had an overnight birthday party. He had a massive front lawn about half the size of a football field, perfectly manicured, and ripe for pitching half a dozen tents. This marked the first time I was invited to a birthday party and everyone actually got along just fine.

Robert became my other best friend that weekend, and we would go on to have weekend hangouts when I couldn't get together with Jake. We mostly stayed at his house because my mom didn't like him because of "woman's intuition."

I never got into trouble with Robert, her "intuition" failed to warn about Henry. He was another sort of frienemy who lived on the other end of our complex. We did a few things, but I was the person used in this relationship. Henry stole some things from my pewter statues, toys, or other things. So, I rarely let him into my house.

I visited his home, and found out a bit of why he was so cruel. Henry's father was a grade-A piece of work. If I knocked on the door, he would open it and point up the steps to his room. He never said anything to me. If I called the house, he yelled to Henry if he was home, but if not and I asked that he tell him I called, he would just say, "I'm not his answering service" and hang up. He reminded me of my mom's boyfriend, William. I stopped seeing Henry in seventh grade after we got into some big trouble together, but that is a story for later.

I met another friend in town, an adult this time. He was the first adult I ever met that talked to kids right. He was a boomerang manufacturer and I would help him sell boomerangs in the Edinboro Mall flea market. I even went out to another flea market in another city with him once. It was a great time, and he was an appropriate friend, a bastion of light in my dark world, but he moved away right after my seventh grade year ended.

I met another good local friend near the end of sixth grade. We weren't able to do much over the summer due to various groundings and vacations on everyone's part. He had the perfect family: a mother and father that were home and available to talk to. He had a younger brother, who was treated the way I wish my brother had treated me. We reconnected in seventh grade because we shared some classes. He was my best friend for the year. Sometimes I stayed the night at his house, and other times he stayed at mine. We mostly shared a love for Legos and board games, but sadly, he also moved out of state right at the end of the school year and I never saw him again.

Moving along into eighth grade, I had finally made some friends among the fellow outcasts. Jake had moved away by this time, though we were still able to see each other on weekends. My Boomerang-making friend and the other boy my age left my life entirely. My local friends were all gone once again, leaving only the frenemies, who started growing distant.

I started burying the many taunts of school bullies deep within myself. I liked attending school to hangout with friends I couldn't see any other time, though my grades showed I didn't do anything academic during the day. Our rag-tag group of outcasts banded together, taking on an identity of the headbangers with our loud music, leather and jean jackets, and heavy metal T-shirts. Our group was complete with the leather-bound chick, a dude that looked just like Elvis, myself, Robert, and two farm-raised brothers who didn't fit in with any other group, so they hung with us.

At school, we feigned toughness, but at home, most of us were raw and hurting. I was left home alone most of the time. My brother was always out with friends to avoid the relational mess developing in our house. Mom was generally at work, at William's house, or at our neighbor's house, probably avoiding the same. I became a recluse, always alone in the home. I isolated myself in my room, darkened the windows with thick blankets and burned incense to Pink Floyd's *Echos* on repeat.

During this period of time, Robert attempted suicide. Our whole group felt the possible sting of death. We were the outcasts, the losers, the people destined to go no where in life. The teachers knew it, our classmates knew it, and there was nothing left to do but be merry and enjoy the pleasures of life, for after all this, we will just die[1].

Robert had another sleepover near the end of eighth grade, and I was among a few kids invited over. I didn't even know it was going to be a group, but when we rode the bus to his house after school on that Friday afternoon, another outcast kid from my neighborhood joined up. An older high schooler was also there, and Robert also invited his neighbor who was in a grade below us.

We walked out into the woods when the Edinboro delinquent pulled out a bag of dried leaves. He passed it over to the high school kid who smelled it and said it was good stuff. They were talking about their weed that had cost ten bucks at the usual drop in the boys room next to the library.

The older boy looked to each one in the group asking if they were going to smoke some. I was the oddball out who actually thought drugs were pretty stupid, so I said I wouldn't be partaking. He started to get threatening about 'NARCing' on him, but Robert had some reasons to both trust and fear me at the same time, so he backed the leader off with his cool humor. I was content with them smoking their weed, I just didn't want to join them.

---

1 1 Corinthians 15:32

One Wicked Sapling

Later that night, the high school cool kid used his experience to teach the middle schoolers how to roll up the joint. The four of them went outside to smoke their weed. It was their first time, and I recall the stupidity of the kids as they tweaked out their high. I actually stood at the upper banister above them and spit on them from above. They thought it was the man on the moon. It was the foolishness of my friends that showed me why I never wanted to use drugs. My conscious self was too important to let it all go under the influence of marijuana.

That night showed me the definition of a real friend. Robert was content to keep me as a friend even though I was his only friend that didn't do drugs with him. We continued being good friends for the next few years, sharing many adventures through the beginning years of high school.

Solitude

October 19, 1995

Staring out with weary eyes
Into the light from darkness
I saw all the children in play
They run with joys of fun
But obscured to darkness
I was stricken to solitude
I thought of entering them
But I divined I should not
Thinking of the droning
Concealed upon my presence
All would taunt me like the rest of them
They knew my supple emotion
They would continue the tease
Like the thrust of a blade
Obliterating my words
From my thoughts of mind
Causing reticence about me

With age comes Wisdom
And the taunting shall end
Elementary mentality leaves
Now all the mocking is innocuous
Causing only loutish behavior
Upon the eccentric one.

Leech

October 14, 1995

The realm of psychedelic colors
Causing emotive to their eyes
Embalming in their minds
And through the sands of time.

Those who perceive it only as a dream
Or take its seduction
They will fail
With lost minds in disproduction

The fearful thrive, with unbroken eyes
To discover a way from there slumber
Living in an unconscious state
Filling their minds with lumber

Only once before, the hue this way
But withdrawn was hate and pain
Only once before when things were safe
Soon all shall lead to bad or good fate.

We lie right down and feel the high
As we look up towards the stellar sky.
Us and old friends beyond our fights
Oh whatever happened, on that summer night.

Your Child's Worst Influence

Mr. T once said, "I might have been born in the ghetto, but there ain't no ghetto in me." He spoke on the importance of personal choices. Bad influences are all around us, ripe for our adoption. When Mom moved us from the dirty city to the clean-cut suburbs, she had no idea that the influences she sought to flee awaited us with open arms, even behind the beautiful facade of our new prissy community. My brother and I were not born in the ghetto, but our life circumstances up to this point infused the ghetto into us.

As soon as we moved to Edinboro, my brother made a new friend. He became a household item during our first summer, hanging out in our unsupervised house while Mom worked day shifts at the nursing home. Mom had given my brother specific instructions that if he left the house, I was to be a tag-along. It was such a bummer for a twelve-year-old to drag along his ten-year-old kid brother into his summer mischief.

On our first adventure we walked to the campus bookstore to get candy. Such a distance intrigued my heart like a beckoning to freedom.

"Who'll pay?" I asked while we walked down the street.

Our new friend was an accomplished shoplifter. He used the time walking to teach us how to shoplift when we made it to the store. Our crash course in the subtle art of theft resulted in A+ work, well, at least more professional thievery than stealing toys from Nathan. This kind of stuff could get us in real trouble, and the high induced by an adrenaline rush made me enjoy the art of stealing as much as the exhilaration of acquiring new possessions.

Poor kids like us enjoyed both. My lessons taught me how to use sleight of hand to submerge a Three Musketeers bar down the front of my pants. We walked around the store for a bit, letting the high of the hide subside before going for a larger, harder quarry: cassette tapes (in 1989, compact discs weren't mainstream enough to be in college bookstores).

Hiding our pilfered confections from our parents was child's play, but the cassette tapes required a deeper plunge into the bag of deceit[1]. Our minds fabricated a story that only a fool could believe: we were walking through the woods and found a bag containing some cassettes. To make our lie more believable, we threw the tape cases across some rocks, inducing scuff marks. Mom bought it. We had learned the art of theft, experienced the adrenaline high, and lied our way out of it, all in one brief afternoon.

For my part, I felt cool. Despite my place near the bottom of the social pecking order, in my own mind, I was a tough kid who graduated from stealing toys at little kids' houses to learning how to increase my tape library and get things I wanted without having the difficulty of work or the problem of money. I'd gained another secret to hide in my heart and another skill to bend to my horrid desires. I got away with stealing again and again, a skill that started a two-year crime wave in the local stores. Hide your cassettes and candy. Here I come!

At the peak of my skills, I walked into the local McCrory's store and pilfered six packs of gum. To throw off suspicions I always bought the seventh pack. After all, nothing induces fear in a store manager more than a regular eleven-year old patron who buys nothing!

---

1 Proverbs 12:20

Your Child's Worst Influence

I wasn't stealing just for me, though. I found that if I had an endless supply of Juicy Fruit, I could pay tribute to the kids who incessantly teased me. My skills were prostituted for the privilege of making friends. I saw no other way to end the taunting, and shoplifting gave me an adrenaline high that made my miserable life more exciting.

Eventually all criminals make mistakes, and after two years, my shoplifting spree abruptly ended. That's what I got for not working alone! Fresh out of sixth grade, and after our first week of grounding, my brother, his friend, and I thought it would be fun to set off some fireworks. Darn! No money and no fireworks. We'd just go to Ames to "pick some up!"

The three of us managed to fill our sleeves and pockets to the brim. We left the store and headed over to the lot behind Giant Eagle to burn off about a hundred dollars worth of stolen goods. We had a blast but it was too little. Rather than be content[1], we went for the excess. Our stupid encore resulted in our bust. I remember seeing a man chase after us when we left Ames the first time, but once we crossed the property line, stopped pursuing us like a pit bull at an invisible fence. He headed back to the store, but he knew exactly who to tail when we walked back in for our encore.

I was stuffing some firecrackers down my pants when I looked up to see a man watching me from beyond a display. I went around the corner to empty my pockets when undercover security busted us. They paraded their captives through the store like a conquered army. Our failed spoils were $30 of fireworks in our hands, shaking with fear. We reached the front office of the store with all eyes watching us go into the security station, including Nathan's mother. Her position as a cashier gave her a front row seat to our busting. The cherry on top of

---
1 **Hebrews 13:5**

One Wicked Sapling

our capture was her sly grin. I know for sure she said to herself, "You reap what you sow, boys[1]."

The store mixed mercy with justice and handed us back to my mother instead of calling the police. They figured at our age we might learn a lesson by being banned from the store for a year. This event stopped my stealing spree. I have never stolen anything else since that day. But the whole situation stole from me the last vestige of my self-respect.

My regret wasn't the mistake of getting caught, nor was it being banned from the local department store. My sorrow came from the way Mom reacted. We had lost all privileges that day for an unspecified period of time. That didn't bother me. The blow was dealt that night before Mom left for her shift. She busted into my room and delivered stern warnings about what might happen if I leave my room before she returned the next morning. Following that, she looked me square in the face and declared, "You are a thief. I hate f---ing thieves." She slammed my door and left. Never had a warm summer night felt so cold.

Not all of my friends needed a tribute of Juicy Fruit. Some of them were just like me. They found my personal belongings to be their tribute. Henry was one such friend. The first time I caught him stealing from me, I didn't allow him back in my house again. While we were in the seventh grade, I still went to his house from time to time because he was in the neighborhood while the rest of my friends were either on the other end of town or in the country to the north. Henry and I never visited stores together, but we did spend a lot of time in the basement of the local apartment buildings.

The apartments had storage cages assigned to each resident. Some of them were empty, but others were full of enticing stuff secured behind inhibiting locks. Henry and his next door

---
[1] Galatians 6:7-8

neighbor looked through the storage cages frequently, and on one occasion, all three of us and another kid on the block went down into the basement.

I had learned my lesson about stealing but knew what they were doing. I didn't leave, but rather, I stood next to them while they did wrong. I had never been taught to be careful of the people I had befriended[1]. Two of the boys took some tools from one of the cages while me and the other kid looked on. One boy acquired a guilty conscience and turned us all in for exploring where we were not supposed to be. He got nothing, but the rest of us were arrested about a week later. Mom took me down to the local police department where I was read my rights. I fully cooperated with the investigation. Even though I didn't steal anything, I was still charged as an accomplice and sent to the firehouse for ten hours of community service.

This situation taught me three life lessons. The first is that persons can be charged for a crime they know has happened if they don't report it[2]. I didn't steal any tools, but I was with the kids who did, so I was guilty. The second lesson is that foolish friends can drag a person down. I needed to be very careful with my associations[3]. Finally, the legal system takes sorry, humble criminals and hardens their hearts. The horrible kids who taunted me in school had nothing on the cruelty of the firemen who treated us as subhuman creatures, worthy of verbal abuse. Perhaps if these "community leaders" showed more compassion, fewer kids might look up to better role models and cease becoming repeat offenders[4]. There must be a balance between mercy and justice.

---

1 Proverbs 4.14
2 Deuteronomy 21.7
3 1 Corinthians 15.33
4 Proverbs 15.1

One Wicked Sapling

I ditched these seventh-grade friends immediately, and eventually summer arrived. My best friend from seventh grade moved away at the end of the school year. Our last sleepover was a bittersweet time of ravaging Legos in the living room until four in the morning. After he left, it was back to the frenemies until I had allegedly shot one of them in the head with a BB gun. I deny such accusations...and if I did do it, it was purely accidental. No one believed my story, and I was grounded again—another summer in the hole!

One morning while Mom slept after her night shift at the nursing home, I was relaxing in an early morning bath when the doorbell rang. Human contact beckoned, so I grabbed a robe and opened the front door. Nobody stood there, but I heard something in the bushes under my brother's window. An older teenager hid behind the cedar, tapping on my brother's window. I knew in a second that I wanted to meet this weirdo. I opened the door and asked who he was.

"I'm Lenny," he said, "is your brother here?"

I let him in and woke my brother on the way back to my bath. Lenny was sitting in the living room when I emerged. While I wasn't allowed to have friends over, I don't remember a rule about enjoying my brother's friends, and the crazier the better!

Lenny ran an underground newspaper in the high school. I was instantly fascinated by his ability to tap a phone and make flammable compounds like Molotov cocktails and napalm. This upstanding specimen of the human race was on the run from the cops for threatening someone with a paintball gun. He thought our house might be a place to hide and that he did. For the better part of a month he lived in my brother's closet only coming out when Mom wasn't home, which meant he had the run of the place. One day when she had a day off from work, she even put clothes away in the closet without seeing him hidden in the random junk present in nearly every high school kid's closet.

When Mom left the house or was asleep, Lenny came out and taught me his ways. I learned about using a phone by tapping the wires together, and I absorbed the lesson about "Fun with Gasoline" from one of his newsletters. I also learned about other things that would make any bank robber proud! Of course, I practiced his arts regularly.

Jake lived on the edge of the community by the lake, so after making a fair amount of napalm with gasoline and flour, I took my cherished black Zippo over to his house and we burned some things back in the desolate keys of Edinboro Lake. It wasn't enough wanton destruction for my taste, so when I found that one of his neighbor kids had access to gasoline I taught him and Jake about how to have their own explosive fun. Surprisingly, no injuries or property damage occurred in the process!

My summer went down in flames, and we moved on to eighth grade. I was a hardened fool by this time in my life, an experienced, yet reformed thief with a criminal record who loved to play with various gasoline-fueled concoctions. I always carried a butterfly knife in school, and I was a paragon of indolence in academics. I even squeaked out a C in gym class! I hated life, school, and most other things. I sought every possible path that might have been taboo. I was your child's worst influence.

Mother

May 19, 2002

If it were a sin,
I was taught to do it
If it took a cheat,
I was taught to win
The truth rarely told,
I was the art of fabrication.

I used these once,
To win my way
And when I was caught,
I was shunned by she who taught me.

Language not fair,
For a boy of so young
Then to stand and turn,
Slam the door and run.
That summer night was warm,
But colder than a winter storm.

I was told to avoid the high,
Though he was always flying
And one day I smelled some herbs,
And he was not home but she.

Then the piercing words,
Of hateful poking fun
To pull me down so deep.

Character Drama sets fast in,
And the Poor Me comes tumbling out
Tries to make me feel,
Guilty for my trying

Your Child's Worst Influence

She's beating down my trust.

God help her see it,
I know that through you
She can come to light
And I can turn to peace inside,
Amen.

No Family Man

Moving to Edinboro, we were transplanted from a neighborhood with kids our own age to one with much younger children. Our conflict in Meadville abounded from the usual frenemies on the block, but we hadn't such an opportunity in our new neighborhood. The closest kid to my age was Nathan, who was three years younger than I was. While I was a shiny new double-digit ten-year old, Nathan was scarcely seven and barely into elementary school. Still, I was the only other candidate for friendship in the neighborhood not in diapers, so his parents reluctantly allowed us to play as long as it was under their watchful eye in their house. They lived in the tan house at the end of the street.

When I told my mom I was going over there and pointed in the vicinity of the house, declaring it to be the 'tan one over there' she nodded consent and I was off. After an hour or so, she went looking for me and happened to stop by the first tan house 'over there' (I neglected to mention there were two of them). Mom knocked on the door asking if I was over there playing her son.

"Not likely. My son's only three," Sally said, a cigarette in her hand.

Mom told her the name of the kid I was with, and Sally pointed further down the block, but not after inviting Mom in for coffee. She accepted the invitation and began one of her longest and most endearing friendships. Sally was similar in age to my mom, and also worked as a nurse, making them excellent gossip partners about the triumphs of their respective medical communities.

Sally started her family a little later than mom did, and probably more by accident than on purpose. She lived with her boyfriend, James, with whom she had two young children. A little girl, five, and the son. Mom always wanted a little girl, and so friendship with Sally gave her adult friendships, and a defacto-daughter without the rest of the responsibility. But the house also gave her an escape from the infighting of her growing boys. It allowed her a place to start openly smoking. As true friends in the ditches of life, Sally and mom smoked like they were on fire and sucked down coffee like they were trying to put themselves out.

Sally and James were classic good people. While their lifestyle was vulgar, they would give you the clothes off their back if they thought it would help. Mom developed her instant kinship, and it was the influence of Sally wanting to give her kids a good time that finally launched our joint vacations, but I am getting ahead the story. Still, James was the only man I knew during these preadolescence years, though he wasn't the best role model.

James was formerly a regular DUI offender reported in the police beat, and by the time we had moved into the neighborhood he moved in with his girlfriend as a means to evade law enforcement. Mom told us that if any police officer stopped us to ask if we know a James in the neighborhood, we were to lie and say we didn't. These months on the run (I never knew when the police matters were resolved), taught him that if he "wanted to catch a buzz, he would do it at home," as he told me many years later.

While James was the only man I ever encountered during my middle school years, he was a personification for what men were in my life: just there. He didn't take any effort to get to know me, not that he should have. He had his own two children and worked full time as a plaster contractor. I knew where he was, but never really talked to him in any serious way. He was nice, but passive. He usually perched himself quietly in a kitchen chair gulping down coffee while Mom and Sally shared work stories. But I was rarely ever there during those years; it was just the place I ran to if I needed Mom for some reason or another, and I tried to need her as little as possible.

Around that first summer, Sally became pregnant again and gave birth to another girl. My mom was named the godmother, and this further solidified an enmeshing between the two families. This girl transcended being a defacto-daughter and became something more: the daughter my mom never had. She quickly usurped any time Mom might have had for us; either by her own desire, or our pulling away in the testing grounds of youth. Still, it was the oddest thing ever when Mom wanted to have family portraits made, and the neighbor's daughter was in the photo with us. We never had family pictures – or even outings – without her.

This inclusion of our unrelated sister caused a rift in the house. As attention was turned almost entirely on the little girl, our own lives and actions blurred out of focus. We increased our delinquency. It was in this environment when I became the neighborhood's most accomplished thief. But in the twisted emotions of adolescence, my brother clued me in on our ultimate opportunities without Mom looking over our shoulders.

It was on a summer day when we were preparing to go to Grandma's house when my brother and I were in the packed up car waiting to leave when Mom had to go over and say goodbye to her 'daughter.' I complained that she was always over at

Sally's house, to which my brother, in his quiet grunt said, "Good. It keeps her out of our hair. Let her have a new kid." He was right. We had no one watching us, no one helping us navigate our twisted lives. We had no guidance, or anyone to ask us how our day went. We were effectively alone.

A single mother has very limited time. Work beckons, and full-time work takes more out of us than just the clocked-in hours. Mom had, however, three distractions outside work. The first was Sally and her new daughter. The second was her own boyfriend. She dated William now for a few years, and we almost never saw him. After the red-neck barbecue in the junkyard, the next time we saw him was when he came over just before we moved from Meadville to patch up the holes Michael had left behind in our rented house.

We also went to his house for a picnic shortly after moving to Edinboro, but he never said a word to us without the prodding of my mother. And when he did finally speak it was to try to tell us we need to 'behave' and 'stay out of trouble.' It was odd and certainly forced. Mom wanted him be a father figure to us, but in my estimation a father figure is more than a grown-up with male genitalia. Once he told us his required speech, my brother and I walked to a little pool hall that was the main attraction in the nearby trailer park. After the awkward moment, we didn't see him again for another three years.

William's house contrasted the hustle and bustle of Sally's house; it was a perfect juxtaposition so that my mom had a place of toddler-chaos to visit, and a place without any kids at all. William's house was her escape, her place to spend with her boyfriend doing whatever they wanted to do, devoid of distractions caused by little kids or teenagers.

Before we talk about Mom's third distraction, I need to take a parenthetical look at the two times I visited 'Strange Dad' during my middle school years. After the time in elementary school when I visited our biological father and got sick, I didn't see him again for about three or four years. I think my brother first reached out to him when I was in sixth grade. He had entered adolescence and wanted to know our father. On one incident, he went off with Dad by himself which pissed off Mom because she didn't have any part on making the plans.

After his private visit the both of us also visited Dad somewhere around seventh grade. By this time, he had a long-term girlfriend and was living with her and her two daughters. They lived in a trailer in Erie, and had significantly more possessions than he had when we visited him as a child. The trailer was as one usually finds trailers: sufficient to live, and neither great nor glamorous, but having other kids around helped ease the transition.

Dad followed his dreams. He was interested in sailing and boating, choosing to ignore some job offers so he could be close to the waters he had grown up on. By this time his own business was starting to pick up enough to start making more local friends in the boating and yachting communities, giving us opportunities to see and ride on some larger boats. Still, we took Dad's little boat out onto the lake and spent a day on the water, swimming in the middle of the lake, far from the beaches, having dove into the water from the deck. We did a small amount of fishing, and enjoyed the day.

The only other memory of that trip was that evening, us kids all watched *Dick Tracy* on television while laying on the king sized bed in the back bedroom while Dad and his girlfriend got drunk on beer in the front room. The weekend was over in a flash, and we returned home.

Somewhere around this time, my brother took another trip to Dad's alone, and never went back. I'm not sure if there was conflict, or some other reason they stopped talking. As for me, one year later, in eighth grade, I would have my last visit with Dad until I would be an adult many years later. There was no conflict, but there was nothing enticing me to keep visiting him. We stopped by to meet an uncle, visited Dad's shop, and did little else. I only remember Dad drinking a lot, and even drinking in the car on the way to take me home.

It was probably the events that happened at home while I was away for the weekend that caused me to become a home body. While I was away, Mom decided it was the opportune time to snoop around my room. Her search warrant yielded much contraband: my black Zippo lighter, lighter fluid, some napalm, and more knives than she even knew I had. Of course this also meant she found my little bag of secret goodies. By this time, mere child's trinkets that were of no consequence.

Parents and teenage rooms are always a touchy subject. I don't begrudge the finding of my objects of delinquency as I look back, but at the time it was a deep violation of my privacy and it also set a stage for us searching her room when she wasn't around.

Yes, I stole my contraband back, and uncovered many other secrets from deep within her closet and under the bed. Still, having my room gone through in periods of time when I was not there was one more reason to stay home more often. So while my brother was more of a socialite, spending time outside the house when able, I was just the opposite. I stayed home, but kept myself locked in the bedroom only emerging for required tasks.

In these days I generally only emerged from my room to scavenge for food. As much as Mom was rarely ever home, she committed to making dinner every day and we usually had meals around a dinner table up until around high school. It was that one redeeming factor which glued the family from total separation. But after dinner it was off to my room and mom likewise disappeared into her distractions.

Her final distraction was in the bedroom to watch soap operas. We had accumulated two television sets by middle school and she devoted herself to always record three programs every day. Hell was to pay if we accidentally messed up the VCR and she missed an episode. General Hospital, All My Children, and One Life to Live consumed her home life. She locked herself in the bedroom for hours at a time watching soaps and crocheting blankets, stuffed animals, and pot scrubbers. The only time I would see her was when she yelled out to bring her a glass of ice water.

Of course, maybe she locked herself in her room because my brother was always out, and I was locked in my room. It was like living in solitary confinement, but the prison door was open. But I was happy in my lonely cell, not wanting to be prodded by the outside world.

It was during this period of time when she started openly smoking in the house. I had personally kicked the habit and I wanted a mom who wasn't smoking so much. Once when we had a school health fair I picked up a lot of "How to Quit Smoking" guides and placed them on her ash trays, on top of her cigarettes, and on her pillow. I think I overplayed my hand because they found their way into the trash can, having never produced a discussion.

My anti-smoking campaign fell on deaf ears in sixth grade when the all-out three way war began. My brother listened to heavy metal at the time and I was still only into Weird Al, so we one upped each other with our little radios.

One Wicked Sapling

Eventually, his music tastes slowly rubbed off as I secretly started adopting some of the heavy metal and hard rock. I hid my secret about my music choices so as to not let on that I was imperfect at my past music choices and vocal declarations about how bad *that* music was. But eventually it became known that I, too, enjoyed some of the bands like Def Leppard, Mötley Crüe, Megadeth, and Metallica. The battle of the stereos drove Mom out of the house more, and sent her to Sally's or William's house where open smoking was more accepted.

Near the middle of eighth grade my brother also started smoking both cigarettes and pot, and I was growing more contempt for him because I held fast that drugs were stupid. Having just experienced the party at Robert's house, wanting as little to do with drugs as possible, I sought escape from my brother, too. Not that I didn't try to argue with him. He would just give me more of his sage logic: "Everyone I know smokes pot, even Mom," he said.

I didn't want to believe him. As tense as my relationship with Mom had been, I wanted to hold fast that there was good in the world and that Mom wouldn't do such a thing, but he presented his case.

"William grows it, and they gave a bunch to James. He showed me the bag."

This drove me into her room to search high and low. I found my knives and lighter, and I found some other hidden things, but I was unable as of yet to find a bag of drugs. I put the thoughts in the back of my mind and plugged along with the final year of middle school. At the end of the year, I came home from school and smelled the pugnacious odor of weed. A surge of contempt for my brother ran through my veins. *Why did he have to light up at home?* I said to myself.

No Family Man

But he wasn't there. I heard a faint noise from the back bedroom, Mom's bedroom, so I walked as quiet as I could down the hall. I stuck my head near the door and heard the familiar tone of General Hospital, and noises of Mom being in there. I got on all fours near the bottom of the door and sniffed the air. The odor emanated from out of her room. Mom was in there getting high, and the last stronghold of defense I had for her started tumbling down. In my heart contempt grew even for her. And there was no one else in the family to take the reigns, I was no family man.

I Don't Care If I Go to Heaven

We often misunderstand the term 'Dark Ages.' Our mindset, mostly informed by stories of knights and sorcerers of old, reflects an era when evil was rampant. Far from meaning evil, however, the term refers to a period of little progress or record. My early middle school years were the dark ages of my soul.

After leaving Tony behind in Meadville, I had no friends, associates, or even acquaintances that I know of who were religious in the slightest. The concept of a church, kid's program, adult studies, or anything resembling a church was totally absent. Likewise, in my comings and goings, I didn't walk by any church buildings as I had in Meadville. My fleshly mind sought nothing more than pleasure, and by whatever means necessary.

I had followed Mom's footsteps, rejecting outright the idea of God. I was a young atheist who neither sought God nor thought I missed anything in life. I subdued any emotions by my conquest's adrenaline. I lived in the here and now, sucking so much marrow out of life that I frequently choked on the bone.

Eighteen months after moving to Edinboro I had my first brush with religion. The "Camp From Hell" I was forced to suffer in fifth grade sent out mailings to all the parents whose kids attended. The summer camp presented a break for Mom, so she shipped her two sons off to the woods bordering northern Pennsylvania and Ohio.

Camp was pleasant during the summer session. My school classmates didn't attend, so I received a reprieve from my reputation and accompanying insults. I forged new friendships in what I perceived was a blank slate opportunity, but I was still the same typical loner. Even so, the adults at the camp included me in the various activities: swimming, hiking, shooting rifles, and using a bow and arrow. It truly was a good time, representing one of the better memories from my childhood.

By design, it was not a religious camp. In fact, our counselor was a late-teen Spaniard who took it upon himself to make sure all his kids could swear in his native tongue, giving us regular drills on our accent and pronunciation in the same way kids in Christian camps were made to recite their memory verses. Still, in the early 1990s it was common to respect religion, so the camp offered a Wednesday and Sunday church service for the kids from faithful families.

We campers were carted off to a chapel in the woods. The warm air cooled as we walked into the trees, candle light illuminating a path showing the way in the fading evening. We had to "be quiet" and "have respect" as we filed into the chapel area that was off limits during our usual daily activities. The wooden benches were hard, and the vibe was like the times I had visited the Catholic Church with Tony, but sadly, I had no material for spitballs with me.

A church service in the woods provided a better environment than the ones I had attended in the past, although the content still bored me enough that I tuned out even before the preacher began his long monologue. I cannot recount his words, but I do remember the service ended with an altar call encouraging kids to come forward to make some kind of "decision". It was at this point in the service that my brother either went forward or at least raised his hand to "accept Jesus" or something like that. On pickup day, Mom received the "great news" that my brother had become a Christian. They gave him a Bible and provided Mom with instructions for finding a good church to nurture his decision.

Neither God nor camp changed my brother. He was the same person after the event as he was before. He discarded the Bible into the trash can, and he never attended a church service until he was married many years later. Even then he was only present because he was the groom. The single immediate effect of the false conversion was that we never attended the camp again.

Other opportunities to reject God soon presented themselves. Like the lame-pawed dog we adopted and named *Gimpy*, the Hound of Heaven would soon send me more fodder to laugh at the absurdity of religious people.

On a summer day shortly after my brother's supposed conversion to Christianity, I rode my bike with Nathan, my brother, and the other frienemy on the block down nearby Hillcrest Street. We were stopped near the intersection at the bottom of the hill by two young men on foot. They were dressed nice, probably more nicely than I was used to seeing in the heat of summer. They were friendly, and we thought they might ask us directions, but instead they wanted to give us directions...to heaven. One of them spoke.

"Do you know if you'll go to heaven when you die?"

We four boys were in a row, I being furthest from the man talking. Each one of us responded in kind, "I don't know."

The hook was dangled before us, and these missionaries were staring down a four-for-one salvation deal through our eight little eyes. Their training took over, "Do you want to be sure you will be in heaven when you die?"

"Yes, yes, yes," came in sequence.

Their eyes fixed on me, but the poor fools were unprepared for my answer: "I really don't care." At least I was both honest and consistent (for probably the first time in my life).

All the training for handing out tracts assumed that no one wanted to go to hell and that everyone longed for heaven. I threw the man off his script, so his emotions took over.

"You know you will burn in hell forever if you don't make it into heaven," he replied, probably counter to his training.

"I don't believe in God, or heaven, or hell," I said back to him.

Thrown off, he left me as a burning branch in the fire. He turned to the other three boys, pretending he wasn't having this conversation, and said to them, "You can be *sure* you will go to heaven if you say this easy prayer. Do you want to say it?"

They said they would and they closed their eyes. Even I said the words with them, and the missionaries declared our position in heaven. They handed us some Bible tracts and told us to find a good church. The missionaries walked off, rejoicing for the four souls they thought they just sprung from hell.

We immediately discarded the tracts in a nearby lawn, and none of us changed anything. Last I knew Nathan became an experienced drug dealer, the other boy came out as homosexual, never caring anything for God. Those two could have changed their ways by then, I suppose, but to this day my brother remains a staunch anti-theist. This encounter, however, showed me the absurdity of some people's belief that merely reciting a few sentences can lead a person to heaven,

I Don't Care If I Go to Heaven

provided there was such a place. We all had a good laugh at the encounter later.

Not that spiritual matters didn't eventually beckon. As we grew, in addition to starting to look toward the opposite gender, our nature also opened up to asking whether there is more to life than the fleeting pleasures of childhood games.

I recall being curious about that as I explored books and television programs about ghosts and aliens. I became keenly interested in the paranormal. In my search I never considered Christianity because I had already experienced enough of that in my past to know it was fake.

Church was long, boring, and pointless. People there suggested that a simple prayer is enough to bring us to an afterlife but their religion didn't seem to inform our circumstances on earth. The church life offered no way to explore and explain difficult questions. I also thought that if there were a God who loved us, why did things always seem to go so wrong for me? I never gave Christianity another thought, but I met certain people who seemed to have some answers pertinent to this world.

Just before the start of eighth grade, Robert invited me to his birthday party again. He didn't have the big camp out as he had the previous year. This event was much smaller with only a few friends, one of whom was Mindy. We all got started talking about the spiritual side of things, and I declared my bold stance that I believed in ghosts and other dimensions, but not in some 'god'. Others shared their views, but when Mindy and I were able to talk more privately, she told me about what she believed. She kept her secret even from her best friend, but she sensed I was open to her ways. Mindy descended from a family of witches.

One Wicked Sapling

I learned much about Wicca and witchcraft that day. My mind opened to see how spiritual forces (not God, angels, or demons, mind you) are real and that those forces sit at our beck and call when we harness magick's[1] power. While I was not specifically interested in practicing Wicca, I did undergo intense study to understand it. The field I was most interested in was white and black magick, which I learned was even more powerful than witchcraft. While witchcraft was about communing with and becoming whole with nature, seeking advice from beyond the grave, magick was about using the same spiritual forces to control the physical world, which was more aligned with my goals.

In the midst of my introduction to magick, I still held a deep-seated morality that I could not explain at the time. But such morality caused me to steer almost exclusively toward the white end of magick, dipping only occasionally into the realm of gray, but never into black. I became drunk on the ability to control physical aspects in my world. Since most of my life was starting to spin totally out of control, any grasp to make my temporal life better was a gamble I was willing to take.

---

1 Magick is correctly spelled with the "k" when referring to the occult practice.

Empty Pleasure in Myself

Sigmund Freud led the forefront of the psychological research which suggested children are inherently sexual. I disagree. While I had experienced my fair share of sexual encounters as a child, I cannot say they were generally enjoyable, nor did I 'seek' them myself. Rather, I was often sought as the tool to pleasure others. It was sickening when those times occurred, but I sometimes repeated the actions with a peer on our terms to better understand my encounters.

When we moved from Meadville where I experienced both the forced participation and the willing experimentation, the opportunity to consider the sexual side of life also faded. My pre-pubescent mind didn't care for such things and as such, I experienced a few golden months of sexual respite where I was neither sought, nor did I seek such pleasures. My focus instead turned to finding ways to protect myself from bullies and seeking hobbies to make me acceptable to the other kids.

My break didn't last long. An older boy in the neighborhood noticed that I was a loner and did not have friends around, so he sought me out. It turned out his pursuit was for his own gratification. It is said by psychologists that we will often stay in abusive relationships because the painful known is less frightening than uncertainty. I was used by this boy in the same way the ones in Meadville had used me, but to a greater extent. Our interactions lasted four years, until the time he found a complicit girlfriend, and I was happy to never see him again.

On Easter the year we moved to Edinboro, he told me that he knows how to touch himself in a way that made him feel good, and he asked if I wanted to learn how to do it. He showed me his skill and the feeling mirrored those I felt when I would climb the poles in the park as a younger child. I was ten years old when I became addicted to touching myself. That provided another adrenaline rush for a child seeking to escape a crazy world. Nearly every night became the time to relax from the stress and pressure of the day.

In the early 1990s pornography was still hard for kids to come by. Sure, the local video store had a dirty section available upon request, and some stores had the magazines available if you were to ask, but they were not front and center. The Internet wasn't yet a thing (I was just about in High School when the first picture arrived on the World Wide Web). Still, where there is a will there is a way. We managed to find a few images. Usually such images came from older siblings. In our case, my brother's best friend was the younger brother, and his older brother had "connections." He hooked us up with some center-folds and a few small clippings. We all looked at the photos which were tame by today's standards. I was more interested in the mix of curiosity, and taken in by peer pressure. That is, after all, what a boy is supposed to *want* to do.

I was granted a few photos of my own to keep hidden away. I stored my photos in a separate place from my other hidden objects (and when Mom found my napalm and knives, she didn't find my dirty pictures). Still, I didn't seek out a lot of photos and I was never addicted to looking at the naked ladies as much as I was in stimulating myself, so my collection was merely one of status and adrenaline rather than of pleasurable use.

Empty Pleasure in Myself

In those days video was the Holy Grail. We could dig through our contacts for a glimpse of girls, but those who acquired moving picture were the envy of boyhood. I was able to view some dirty movies when my brother had friends over, and everyone was watching them under the privacy of their own blankets. I was pretty sure I knew what they were doing. I found my own collection of X rated movies by 7th grade after receiving a shiny new 13 inch color television for Christmas that year. I quickly used my savings to buy my own private VCR.

Now having a private viewing room, I quickly set out on a quest for the Holy Grail. I procured my video tape from Robert who used his connections in Erie. Now I was the cool kid in our little group. I had the collection, but the envy was television, a VCR, and a private bedroom.

Still, with a movie collection, I didn't become addicted to the pornography and I rarely ever watched the films. Bragging rights were my interest. I was the one with a video collection, and I showed it off when needed. I acquired my photos and video tapes before I naturally took any interest in girls.

I was a very late "bloomer," not beginning the journey of adolescence until around 8th grade. Just before this, Robert's friend Shelia, whom he knew from Erie, was interested in going on a blind date. We talked on the phone quite a bit and one day we had the chance to meet up at the Millcreek Mall with my brother and Lenny coming along as well. We three youngsters took the bus into the city and met Robert, Shelia, and Mindy for a day of teenage exploits.

On meeting Shelia she found that I was an awkward boy not yet interested in girls. She looked for a way to dump me for Lenny instead, so she made up a story that I kept pushing her away during the movie. Her story was a farce, but I was more interested in the movie than the things she wanted to do. Still, we went our separate ways, and I returned to my own evening releases.

It was only a few months later that I would begin the journey from which we never return. I finally understood the pleasures, the exploits, the opportunities, why Shelia wanted another guy, and even why the neighborhood boy did what he did. During these times, my self-abuse sky-rocketed and I became afraid of people, assuming they all wanted to use me. I retreated back to my empty pleasures in myself.

A Journey Down the Wide Road

Enter through the narrow gate;
for the gate is wide and the way is broad
that leads to destruction,
and there are many who enter through it.
Matthew 7:13

Father Knows Nothing

It has been said that a stable family provides roots for a young person to grow up confident. Maybe the antithesis of such a statement explains why my life was full of hate, arrogance, and turmoil. By the end of eighth grade, I had begun my journey inward until I became a recluse. My grades consisted of Ds and Fs, except for the C I managed to squeak out in gym class.

I coped at home by blocking out all light from my bedroom window with thick blankets stapled to the wall. I removed the bright white bulb from my overhead light, replacing it with a dim red one. I burned incense and looped Pink Floyd's *Echoes* all day. I gave up all hope in life. I had no one to point me in any direction. I was fatherless, mostly friendless. I felt family-less as my brother always went off to get high with his friends, and Mom sought time at Sally's or William's houses when not at work.

After the November visit with my biological father when I was in eighth grade, I didn't pursue seeing him anymore. Mom always hated him, so she didn't push the issue. William always kept at a distance from our family, except for Mom. I don't recall seeing him at all during middle school, though I am sure we probably met in passing a few times. I certainly never talked to him or did anything with him. It was the same with James down the street. I knew he was there, but we never really talked. My friends had started to fade off into the distance as many of them pursued drugs. I had no interest in losing control of my faculties.

I had just begun ninth grade when Larry, an older friend of my brother, had moved into the house for a while. Mom didn't mind him being there, and he brought groceries home from the store where he worked, so in a way, he paid rent in food. Like me he was a home-body. He had not always been. Larry had traveled with a band during his first year out of high school, even opening for Pearl Jam one summer. He had witnessed the dirty underbelly of the rock and roll scene but decided it wasn't for him.

While he chain-smoked and drank occasionally, he stood against other drugs. We became good friends during the time he stayed at our the house, and he became the second older person (behind the boomerang maker) who treated me well. Larry gave me good advice, and didn't want to use me as a tool to gratify rotten pleasures. He became a mentor of sorts – an inoculation against the influences my heart screamed out to avoid.

Around the time Larry moved out, my brother introduced me to another friend. Bob was the opposite of Larry, a consummate failure in life: approaching thirty he didn't have a real job, a driver's license, a high school diploma, or any direction in life other than gravitating to his next existential delight. He preached the merits of getting high, pursuing any form of sexual expression available, and anything else that progressed the party life. Bob was bad in all the ways that Larry was good. While Bob gave me attention when most others ignored my existence, the attention existed only to gratify his lust.

Meeting these two men provided a conflict in my mind. One of them demonstrated maturity beyond his years while the other behaved like the rest of the immature fools in high school. The mental conflict they provided set the stage for the confusing high school years ahead of me. They shaped, for better or worse, the direction my next few years would take.

In the middle of the summer after tenth grade, I received news from Mom that Michael was down in Pittsburgh for work and had asked to come up for a visit. Other than a package or two he'd sent over the last eight years, I didn't have any contact with him. I said I would like to see him, so Mom and I met at his hotel room in town.

After dinner, Michael and I planned to meet again the following day. Our connection reestablished itself as if no time had passed at all; he was like a father to me. We spent the day in Erie, had some lunch out, bought CDs, and listened to music. We also had a heart-to-heart about the past. He knew the wrongs he did to all of us and he sought forgiveness, which I was glad to extend.

The following day he met Jake and me for lunch, and we talked about the rebellious things teenagers often do. We laughed at funny moments in the past that I was finally old enough to hear about, and then we went home. A momentary lapse of destruction started at this visit and it infected the rest of my summer with hope, but he left the next day. At least we had exchanged phone numbers, so we talked nearly every few weeks afterwards.

After talking to Michael on the phone for a while, he invited me to California for the Thanksgiving holiday in my senior year. It was a series of firsts for me. On the trip, I took my first plane ride, saw the ocean, and visited a mall so big that we only saw half of it in two days. The trip changed my life in many ways. It pierced my heart deeply in that I came to the understanding that I had a father, just one too far away to visit on a regular basis. Long distance relationships are fabulous in one way, but empty in another.

Once I started eleventh grade, Mom decided she wanted to make some changes. Grandma had died the previous summer, and my brother moved out right around this time. Grandma's estate came to a close, but Mom's brother finagled things to take the inheritance for himself. Mom hoped for a better future, so she proclaimed her intent to marry William and that we would all buy a house together. We started looking for houses down old roads that society had long forgotten. We found two prospects, each in the sticks flanking the north and south of Meadville. We settled for the one in Saegertown, just eleven miles from our current home.

While I only had a few friends at school, I didn't want to be the new kid again, so I agreed to move with the only condition being that I would not change schools. We changed my legal address (as far as the school was concerned anyway) to Sally's house, and since Mom worked in Erie at the time, she dropped me off there in the morning on the way to her shift so that I could catch the bus to school. This meant I had nowhere to go after school until Mom's shift was over (Sally's house was too chaotic for me), so I generally hung out with Bob for the rest of the day.

We all moved into a huge house in the country. The move was initially exciting for me because I learned about herbology and grew interested in planting my own herbs and vegetables. The land in the country had ample garden space for everyone to have their own plot, and I spent hours planning the perfect garden. I selected the herbs and the other plants and looked forward to a summer of gardening, but it seems life never works out the way we plan. The summer morphed into living in the house from hell.

William's ailing mother moved into the front half of the house. She was a lonely old lady turning senile and had no respect for anyone's time or privacy. Between William and his mom, they had nine dogs: three Doberman Pinschers, a Boston Terrier, two Chihuahuas, a Basset Hound, and two mutts.

Seven of them lived in the house, and unfortunately, one of the dobermans was chained right outside my bedroom window. It had the propensity to whine and howl all day long. Life with dogs during the school year wasn't all that bad since we left early in the morning and never returned until after six. Summer however turned into a thing of nightmares for a kid who grew up in suburbia.

Our first summer lacked the exciting luster my mind fabricated. Mom and William left early each morning to go to their respective jobs, but I was stuck in the house that time forgot. Worse, they marooned me with a senile woman who would open the bathroom door if she thought you were in there.

I once came downstairs to find her endlessly shuffling through our cabinets. I was also stranded with the nine dogs, so I got out of the house to invest in plotting my garden, but that never takes long when most of the time is spent waiting for things to grow.

I escaped into the woods to write philosophy and poetry, but solitary confinement is overwhelming even for an introvert. So I took to riding my bike eleven miles down the road just to visit the thriving metropolis of Edinboro. Population: more than "Hickville".

It helped that during this time I played *Magic: The Gathering*. I often headed to the little card shop to join in on large eight-person games that had spontaneously emerged at the provided tables.

Living with William was like being in a prison camp with a pissed off, unstable warden. He lacked communication skills and had his own 'man cave' even before such a thing was in vogue. He set up a room with all the furniture from his old house that Mom didn't allow in the rest of her living spaces. That room was off limits to the rest of us. The few times he emerged from it, he sat at the kitchen table smoking Winston cigarettes and enjoying a daily Diet Coke and Fudge Round.

Six weeks after we moved to Saegertown, the honeymoon phase of the new blended family wore thin. Mom bought a very expensive massaging rocking chair for William to use in the living room. She could not contain her smile as the delivery men carried the chair in and set it in front of the television. The pride over her gift lifted her into a floating bubble.

William sat in the chair and grunted. Mom turned on the vibration causing William to yell, "It's f---ing vibrating my a--!" and he got up, stormed into his room, and slammed the door. Mom's bubble burst, and she went to her own room to cry over the lack of appreciation of the gift, the wasted money, and the jerk she had married.

The conflicts continued as William oozed jealousy over Mom having friends. She wanted to stop by Sally's house to visit from time to time, but William had instructed her to be home if she was not working. The conflicts became worse, and Mom often told me about their fights as we drove to Edinboro in the mornings for school. Probably the best relationship I developed with Mom in this phase of my life was uniting against a common enemy.

I walked through the school year into spring on pins and needles. William's room lay directly under my own, and if I made any noise at all, he would either pound on the walls or yell profanities up to me. The summer conflicts between Mom and William grew worse. By the middle of the summer he had threatened me with violence, and Mom did nothing about it. Jake wasn't allowed to come over any more (his parents didn't trust William), and somehow, weed killer was thrown on large portions of my garden.

An emotional explosion occurred one day that summer when I mowed the lawn later than William wanted. He was obsessive about when things got done. He tasked me with mowing two parts of the yard, but doing those parts the day before or the day after he did his was not acceptable. That meant I had to give up my time playing cards on the weekends when more people were around. Still, on this Saturday, I was working on my garden when William yelled about needing the rest of the lawn mowed.

I said I would do it when I was done with a section of the garden, but that was not good enough for him. Apparently he said something to Mom because she came out with a bag, wearing only a T-shirt and underwear, and told me to get into the car. We drove off to her friend's house where I slept on the couch until morning. We were like rebels fleeing oppression, but we went back the next morning, and I finished my mowing.

The conflicts only grew worse and more violent, so a week later we left for four days. I stayed the first night at a friend's house, then we went to Sally's for the next three nights. During this stay I picked up a case of food poisoning and had to expel sickening wastes from both ends in someone else's bathroom. The feeling of not having a home was hardening my heart. We got in the car, me still being sick, and debated on where to go next as Sally's hospitality waned. We ended up back at the house from hell for another two months.

Near the end of October, Mom rented a small cottage in Edinboro with a man she had met at work. Unlike William, he was a really nice guy, but he only stayed for a few weeks before leaving the cottage to live elsewhere. I wished he had stuck around. He was better for all of us than William. In this cottage I finished high school and started my college journey. The slightly more peaceful living situation was a capstone of peace in my last year of high school; a reprieve from the prior three years of chaos. Still I never felt at home either there or in the old house.

Ashes to Ashes, Dust to Dust 2

October 13, 1995

I now have seen
With a gleaming gleam
The two sides of the tale
Without a fail
One of good, one of bad
Adversity, to make me mad
They both instructed me
With my senses to see
To listen to both sides of the tale
Without a fail
The good one told me
The good key
What was done
For all his fun
And the pain
And of the fame
But how it had
Even though sad
Destroyed his past life.
The bad one told me
To have fun and to see
What intoxication's
And sensations
Would do for me
For it would
"Open up your senses to see"
I never thought an answer so sought
Would be so inscribed on my mind
I now see what was done for me
One push, one pull
For the trail to stroll

A Journey Down the Wide Road

One let go
And then so
His good path I followed
My scrutiny for destruction
And angers deduction
It's safe to abet
On foot they set
From my mentality
Back to their hostility
Never again to return.

Academic Excellence

My Eighth grade year ended with barely passing grades despite the various aptitude tests indicating my brain cells showed signs of intelligent life. Nevertheless, I had given up on life at this point. Daniel Goleman wrote in *Emotional Intelligence* that regardless of how smart a child is, if their life is falling apart, they don't care enough about the solution to 3 + 3 to even wager an attempt. My life up to now perfectly illustrated his point.

My academic (dis)achievements led to my ninth grade placement in the "Learning Lab" which I described as "special ed for people who are not really retarded." In technical terms, it was a glorified study hall where the rest of the teachers reported directly to the Learning Lab director, so she could be sure to check my assignment book for accuracy. The director signed off on all the assignments as I presented them; I experienced a total reversion to elementary school. The teacher even gave us golden stars for finishing our work, then we could play for the rest of the period! Learning Lab was the dictionary definition of condescension.

The class afforded me a placement in a new university program called CHOICES, which was likely an acronym spawned from the mind of a grad student somewhere. The after school program took me out of my last class of the day twice a month.

A school bus drove us to the Miller Center on the Edinboro University campus to meet with a group for games and talking.

Each group included an elementary age child, a high school student, and a college volunteer. The enrichment program sought to give the elementary and high school students a better outlook on life by pairing us with a volunteer who made college life look cool.

The third grade elementary girl in our group reminded me of myself at that age; nice but awkward. We all talked, played some games on par with the younger kids abilities, and not much else I can recall. The hippie-type college student in my group liked candle making, of particular interest to me because candles are a part of magick. She gave me a catalog of supplies that I found enjoyable to flip through, though I never put it to any use.

On the way back from the EUP campus early in the program, one student asked our van driver, a college volunteer, to stop by the local convenience store to buy her a pack of smokes. By this time, I started giving up on life and my defenses worn down by mom, my brother, and Larry all being smokers. *Cigarettes are not weed, so why not*, I reasoned in my mind. I bummed a few smokes and asked Larry to pick me up a pack of my own next time he worked. I wanted to pick up the cool habit again.

The pack of smokes and lighter fit nicely in my leather jacket pocket, and I smoked about half the pack before Jake convinced me again about how stupid it was to smoke. My defenses redrew themselves and I tossed the remainder of the cigarettes into my brother's room so he could smoke the rest of the pack. I quit again for the last time.

The school year ended with my grades holding low Cs with the occasional B and D in the mix. The Learning Lab issued a final exam derived, I am convinced, from a third grade language placement bureaucrat. One question included, "What color is the sky: Red, Green, Blue, or Yellow." Twenty of the most condescending questions I have ever seen in my life convinced me of the stupidity of the Learning Lab. While the school recommended I keep it, mom listened to my objections and vetoed their request to enroll in the class the following year.

Tenth Grade started like ninth grade ended; I had no real goal, no direction, and a lack of motivation. My brother had a car now, so mom said he should give me a ride to school, but was furious to find him charging me gas money.

I started despising my brother in his last year at our house because his whole life turned into one big party. I held firm on my belief that drugs were stupid, but he picked up his friend from the sticks, way beyond our little borough limit, and they rolled up the windows to get high on the way to school. They tried getting me high off the second hand smoke, causing my hatred for them to fester.

Not that the times getting a ride to school were all bad. We stopped by the gas station in the mornings to get coffee on the way. Showing up to first period Music Theory was more enjoyable with a warm brew in my hands. Ultimately, I eventually went back to the bus because my brother drove like a lunatic and kept trying to get me high. We mostly started staying out of each other's way in the last few months of the school year.

As for school itself, I still had very few friends, and barely even any acquaintances. For lunch, I sat at a table with my brother. In spite of our differences, we were both headbangers and had the same general group of associates. I plodded along the first half of the school year pondering the meaning of life.

My discussion with the guidance counselor likely became my catalyst for change. For the first time in my life, someone looked at me with all my laziness and faults, and without judging, showed me the results of tests indicating I was certainly capable of better work than I exhibited.

I somehow knew this, but with everything around me falling apart, I really didn't care to do any better. Still, the conversation brought to my mind the lack of examples in my home life. I had no father, no mentor, and barely a mother. I realized my home life didn't provide any solutions, so I figured trying anything new would probably be a step up from either doing nothing or following the lifestyle modeled at home, which I despised. I made the conscious choice then and there to dive full-force into academics. I had nothing to lose but a world to gain.

My tenth grade biology teacher said that half-way through the year, it was like a light turned on in my mind. I went from being a lazy student to one who was highly motivated. I completed my work early and seemed to suddenly care about school. Overnight, I rose to the top position in all my classes gaining a deep respect for the teachers, all of which seemed to notice my heightened performance. I ended the year on the principle's honor roll. I looked back over my last few years in school wondering why I made it harder on myself than it actually was. High school education, it seemed, boiled down to nothing more than being conscientious about doing schoolwork.

I grew to love academic pursuits, and with the end of the year approaching I determined myself to continue studying something over the summer. Bob had given me a book on herbs, and so I started reading that from one end to the other. Outside the required school reading (which I still rarely ever finished), John Lust's *The Herb Book* became the second book I ever read (my sixth grade reading of *Misery* was an excellent metaphor for my early life).

I was hooked on natural medicines and herbology. The rest of my summer was spent reading books and going into the woods collecting plants and experimenting with teas, infusions, and other lessons taught in the various readings I examined over the summer. I also committed myself to learning the common and Latin names for all the plants I encountered in the woods.

My study over the summer gave me a new appreciation for learning, and I soon discovered that all knowledge is interconnected. I took to learning with a simplicity resembling teaching basic arithmetic to college math majors. I soared to the top seat in all my classes, and teachers often had to throw out my scores if they wanted to grade on a curve because I kept breaking them. School became so easy for me that I often studied personal subjects of interest during class time and still managed to learn the course work better than my peers. I became academically unstoppable.

The smart kid in class has different challenges than the fool, especially when the students notice the teacher paying special attention to the "pet". All of a sudden, the kids who spent the last several years bullying and teasing me all wanted to be my "friends" so they could see my homework. The ones who pushed me into being an outcast at the edge of sanity, now wanted something from me.

Unlike my sixth-grade self who bought my friends with stolen gum, the new me didn't care for friends at all. I wasn't even interested in being nice. These kids pushed me to the edge of my sanity, and my mind looked for revenge. I became slow and calculating with my answers to their request to see my work. "Maybe in a bit," I said. Of course I never intended to give them any help. They got a kick out of watching me struggle in my younger years, but I lorded my knowledge over my classmates as my personal pride reached paramount proportions. I took pleasure in pushing people away.

One group I finally got along with were teachers. I found that all the teachers my brother warned against taking classes with were actually really nice when students paid attention, did their assignments, and participated. Playing the politics of the schoolyard served me well, and having teachers as friends gave an extra level of protection, and even served me into the future when many of them gave me recommendations for college and even some job references. One of them—my brother's arch-enemy—became a good friend of mine, and we even traded herbs for our respective gardens.

I was not particularly humble in their presence however, and it is a miracle any of them actually liked me at all. In English class while we read *The Hounds of Baskerville*, the teacher pointed out the hemlock trees as foreshadowing of death, being poisonous and all. However, being very knowledgeable on plants and even more arrogant, I corrected her. She still said I was wrong, so the next day I brought hemlock tea made from the needles of the evergreen tree, and I showed her the difference between poison hemlock (a plant in the mustard family) and Eastern Hemlock (the tree in the story). She hated to admit when I was right.

I engaged our environmental biology teacher as well. She was certainly more open to be corrected. On a field trip to Presque Isle in Erie, the senior year students chaperoned the freshman. She pointed out to the edge of the embankment across a bay and asked the students what trees those were (hint: the pioneering species). They were quick to yell out, "Cottonwoods!" She happily smiled, until I looked at them and said, "No, those are Willows...but that is still a pioneering species!" She looked again and gave me a curious glance, correcting herself to her ninth grade class. The respect for my knowledge likely came because this was the third class of hers I had, and the first time I had her in seventh grade, she passed me with a D–, probably to not have to deal with me again.

My studies turned so well I had the opportunity to skip my senior year of high school. I planned ahead in my junior year and took all my last two years of classes at the same time and still managed straight A's on everything.

Despite having full approval to skip, for some reason unknown to me at the time, I didn't end up leaving high school early. I showed up to my last year in high school with only needing a single elective credit to graduate. I willingly stocked up on mathematics and biology, took a full year of early release, and became a teachers assistant and took an independent study.

During the school year in addition to my classes. I personally studied Latin, herbology, natural medicine, learning theory, and some other scattered subjects. I also actually had a few friends in this final year, though I have lost touch with all of them since then.

Beliefs
October 24, 1999

Somehow, from deep within
A beast of greater power came
The mind set was eradicated,
But slowly, like a phase,
The difference was to subtle,
But relative it showed.

After time, yes only time,
Even less than could conceive,
It changed everything, everywhere,
I am alone, but I don't mind,
I wish I could help all on my mind,
They used to want it, but now,
I don't think so.
I lay forth the warning,
But in another language it seems,
That beast sure did a wonder,
I am not the same.
I used to put forth effort,
I really used to try,
But now I don't,
And I still succeed.
From where does it come?
The beast will only know.
How long will it last?
The beast will only know.

I've seen his potential,
I heard his cry,
I came to find he only wanted.

Perhaps I desired.
He only asked.
Perhaps I searched.
He only cried.
Perhaps I stopped.
He only wished.
Perhaps I looked for how.

The mind was the final potential
The barrier to all things,
But perhaps I found that this was true,
Yet only in part,
For the mind has no boundaries.

If only he could see.
If only I could try.
If only he could think.
Not leave it up to me.
If only I could dream,
of what he could become,
but put it in his head,
Instead of mine.
If only he could take this,
And dream it to be true,
If only he could believe,
Believe in himself,
Then perhaps, only then,
He would find he has
The potential he wants.
Believe, and all things
are possible.

Learning to Hate the World

Eighth grade ended and my first summer after childhood began. My struggles in middle school with friends, enemies, drugs, and sexuality dissolved any innocence and naivete from my mind, and I confronted the world boldly behind my insecure heart. I had exactly one friend whom did not smoke or use drugs. It appeared my mom, brother, neighbors, and other friends all gave up on life, so my direction likewise faltered.

Band camp was my summer's misery. To continue on in any of band courses required a year of marching band. I was thus forced to give up my first week of summer vacation, in addition to the last two weeks, not to mention our weekends for the first half of the school year. I guess the powers that be assumed we approached extra-curricular activities with joy.

The first week of band camp gave me a taste of high school, and I wanted to spew such things from my mouth. Perhaps my past pains matured me, perhaps I hated seeing people having fun. Regardless, I saw a group of people who acted so immature that it made me sick. The drum line pretended to incessantly be involved in a giant orgy, and child-like antics manifest themselves in nearly every comment and group activity. Of course, as freshman, we were treated like dirt all week.

The upperclassmen told us we had to do what they said, including forcing push-ups, cleaning up messes, and other small tasks to impute into them a sense of power. Their behavior resembled *The Lord of the Flies*. They banded into groups, teased the outcasts (as a headbanger, I was one of them), and engaged in generally unruly behavior while the adults looked on in indifference.

The conflict came to a head on the last day of "Initiation Week." Robert planned to stay over for the night, so his parents dropped him off at the school to ride home with me at the end of the day. Our group's leather-bound chick, Shannon, was a drummer and so the three of us enjoyed a lunch of pizza and soda when a senior student came over and inverted the garbage can right next to us.

"Pick that up," he said, directing his command to me.

I laughed, shook my head, and said, "You dumped it out, you pick it up."

He snarled in my direction and repeated the order to Shannon. Her milquetoast outlook on life compelled her obedience. She slowly picked up the garbage and refilled the can. He yelled again, "You're picking it up too slowly! Give me twenty push-ups!"

Shannon got on the ground and assumed the push-up position, but Robert objected. He pulled out a small pocket knife, flashing it in front of the kid's face. Robert was the first in our class to make it to the principal's office...a week before the school year began! Mom had to pick up his knife from the principles office and promise to tell his parents about what had happened.

Prior this time Mom always hated Robert, but she never gave any reason for her disdain except "women's intuition." Now, she lorded concrete reasons over my head for why I should leave behind my best friend in school. Still, as much as she rejected Robert as a friend, she let me make the decision about him, so we kept up a good friendship throughout the summer and into the next school year.

Learning to Hate the World

I picked up another short-lived friend from the back woods for the summer and into the next school year. He lived a ways down past Robert's house, down in the country and next to a cemetery. They owned a huge plot of land, had a cabin on the back part of the property, and a giant zip line starting at the top of the steep hill going down into the field and past a creek.

His house was one of the best we saw, and since Mom didn't object to him as a friend, several of us often met over there rather than at Robert's house. Robert and two other McKean friends were all from the same general block of back woods, so often we had a few adventures at his house, but near the end of the summer he too started focusing a lot more on drinking, drugs, and parties. Since I didn't partake of the pharmaceuticals he rarely invited me back.

Jake and I also met up several times over the summer, though he was in a different school district now. He would come over for a long weekend every other week or so until we moved, and I also visited his new rented house on a farm with a big barn to pass time in. Neither of us were into drugs, so we mostly just talked, played video games, or ran around the woods on his property.

We both enjoyed various Nintendo games and *Dungeons and Dragons*, a game we started playing together back in seventh grade. We spent a little time in the woods and a lot of the time at his house messing around in the barn, jumping into piles of hay.

Once I moved to Saegertown he was still permitted to come up so long as Mom was able to drive one direction. His times at my house were brought to a sudden close one day. William, ever the taskmaster, decided that with me and Jake around we should be put to work. It wasn't simple chores, but posting fences and other harder labor.

Jake was holding the fence posts up while I hammered them into place, but I missed and hit his hand, driving it into a tooth on the fence post. We ran inside to see to the blood, but William just yelled at me to get back out there, "We lost one, now I need you to go organize the barn."

William never stopped to help, check on him, or take any other action resembling human compassion or even responsibility. Jake called his parents who had to drive an hour to pick him up and take him to an urgent care center. When his parents asked that we help pay the bill, William swore at his step father and hung up the phone. Jake was never allowed over again.

In our high school years we starting spending more time down town. Edinboro consisted of a bowling alley with *Mortal Kombat II*, a video store, and a mall with zero attractions. My brother hung around his friends and sometimes I followed, especially the time when Mick came to visit for several weeks and I tagged along to experience the summer high school life.

By this time in small town 1990s, friend groups splintered off into titles. The 'Preppies' included the good students from usually nice homes who always dressed nice and sought to tease the outcasts. The 'Jocks' in our town usually avoided the other kids. Most of our local jocks were your best friends if you played sports, but generally ignored you the rest of the time. They were nice to everyone on the occasions they were forced to interact.

The 'Skaters' were a new breed of kids that started emerging as a weird cross-breed of preppie and outcasts. I guess they simply had enough of being goody two-shoes and adopted some grunge from us headbangers, who of course wore either jean jackets or leather, even into the scorching heat of the summer as if it was our armor to protect us from the world.

We ventured into town one summer night and found ourselves walking down the small road near the bowling alley when a whole group of the preppie kids came around and surrounded us. Many of them had been drinking and were drunk on power as well as booze. A skater kid who was good friends with my brother came up and joined ranks with us. While we were out numbered about five to one, Mick, who was a body builder, and the skater, a black belt in karate, boosted our confidence.

My brother told me to go into the "lanes" and tell a guy named Cas that we had preppie problems outside. What I didn't expect was that Cas was friends with everyone on the pool hall side of the bowling alley, and I was followed out with about twenty mostly drunk country guys (don't ask me why, but country hicks and headbangers always got along well). The tides suddenly turned when now our group of guys severely outnumbered the high school bullies. We parted ways, the hicks went back to their pool, and we went home; everyone avoided a fight that night.

That night I saw that the kids who had innocently enough teased and ridiculed me over the years would start fights with anyone they didn't like. I grew in my hatred for those kids, and as a defense mechanism, I put on an evil persona, cut my arms with razors to show how tough I was, and scowled at anyone who got too close.

During these early high school years, mom went back to working third shift, so our house became the teenage delinquent hangout zone. Jake would come over on the weekends, but we mostly locked ourselves in my bedroom to avoid breathing in the poisoned air. My brother had about half a dozen or more friends over nearly every night, and they would smoke so many cigarettes and so much pot that a plume of smoke filled the upper six feet of airspace. Even leaving the room for a brief trip to the bathroom became a hassle.

Our evening was spent in my room listening to Pink Floyd while putting up fluorescent fishing line that glowed in my black light. Eventually my brother started bringing his friends into my bedroom to trip on acid because the shapes were all over the walls and ceilings causing intriguing patterns that mystified their drug-induced mind.

It was one of these parties that I considered trying acid. Jake was not over that weekend so I was left to my own defenses. My brother invited a new friend over but he excluded the rest of the people that usually joined in on the party. I hung out in the living room to meet this new guy. My brother was dropping his first acid that night and this guy would deliver it.

The purveyor of pharmaceuticals destroyed all stereotypes the schools always taught about drug dealers. Rather than a straggly, dirty guy, he was probably the best dressed and clean cut guy I ever met. His smooth complexion gave him an innocent look juxtaposed with slicked back dark brown hair giving him a hint of perplexity. He sat at our kitchen table and reached one hand into his black leather jacket retrieving a package of acid wrapped in aluminum foil. Then he tossed a 9mm gun on the table with the other hand. Now this is a recipe for an interesting evening!

The drug dealer was the nicest guy I ever met. He wanted a head count on the number of hits to prepare and politely asked if I was participating. I said I would not, and unlike the high school "experienced" pothead from my first experience with weed a couple years earlier, he didn't give me a threatening tone. He only said to let him know if I changed my mind. He asked what music I liked and told me about a few other bands I might be interested in, but after a half hour of talking, it was time to take the hit. He instructed my brother on the fine arts of dropping acid while I watched, learning the art myself from afar.

Nothing changed for the first thirty minutes, but slowly the drugs took effect and everyone under the influence started behaving as the whole world transformed into a show. They laughed at everything, described the things they saw: a merry-go-round full of goblins in the back yard, the crawling cheese on the pizza, the living flowers guarding the house, and more. The whole house overflowed with hilarity and everyone enjoyed themselves...except me.

I retreated to my room, on the fence about trying acid. Why was I always the most miserable? Why was I never the one having fun? I pondered these questions listening to Pink Floyd's *The Wall* with my headphones, absorbing the sounds. The first few songs and I wanted to partake. The next few songs, I was not sure. I teetered on my opinions until the chorus of children called out, "We don't need no education, we don't need no thought control..." I was struck with a deeper strength. I wanted to be able to tell kids that it is possible to live life without drugs. My strength was found and so I decided to head back out into the party.

I opened my bedroom door but the house was dark. My first thought is that everyone left, but I saw the dealer's truck still in the driveway. I heard a whimper from the corner. My eyes were already adjusted to the darkness, where I could make out a shivering blanket. I called out only to be met with a scream of terror. The fun was over and the nightmare began.

Everyone took their positions in the dark silence. The overwhelming lights and sounds of the party became too much, driving them all to madness. Escaping colors, escaping sounds, they all became prisoners to their own minds and sought the solitude of quiet darkness. They huddled apart from one another having still six hours left in their trip. This scene is so burned into my mind that I am glad to have never partaken in drugs at all.

The experience further fueled my arrogance and pride. I was able to resist temptation and keep my whits about me while all others fell to the stupidity of drugs. I distanced myself further from the party scenes and watched all the friends from my early high school-days fade away, save for Jake, who by eleventh grade was not allowed to come over. I personally grew a deep contempt for the world.

In tenth grade, I was rarely invited to go to Robert's house because his whole life devolved into drugs. I was not interested in such things. *Magic: the Gathering* became my connection to the world. I received a starter pack as a Christmas present and this allowed me to play some pickup games at school with some of the other kids who played. For the rest of tenth grade and into the summer myself and a few other kids played a lot of cards and it became a good release for the struggles in life. Maybe one can say it kept me from going over the edge.

In my junior year we moved to Saegertown, which was isolated, but school allowed for the occasional game. I grew fond of the bookstore in town that was big on selling the cards and they had tables to play with the other customers. The real problem came in the summer when I became isolated in hickville, causing me to eventually ride my bike to either Edinboro or Meadville to play cards at the game shops there.

Magic was not all good, however. The game has the propensity to be both addictive and expensive. Like crack cocaine (and sometimes it is referred to as Cardboard Crack), the drive to play better means to buy better cards and build better decks. Also, a player needs to stay on top of the release cycle and get the cards as they come out...and at least four copies of the cards, which at that time could still be $20-30 apiece. I was overall a good player even though nearly all of my expendable money went to buying cards.

I stopped playing at the beginning of my senior year of high school when I took second place in a tournament. I progressed up the ranks with an unstoppable white solider deck to play in a tribal tournament. The winner was to receive a box of the latest expansion set, but the judge ruled against my using a tapped Combat Medic (which any player can confirm the ability is able to be used while tapped). The ruling went against me and for the judges best friend, who subsequently won the box.

This showed me that even in a simple card game, favoritism runs wild. I stopped visiting the card shop and stopped playing cards, relieved that I was no longer spending so much money on cardboard. But this also meant I withdrew into myself and having one more reason to hate the world.

Lost Silent Demise
November 14, 1998

Bluish up above turns red,
Dark dome caving in,
A ceiling forms from deep within,
Calling in a final grin.

Tightness in the abdomen,
Effects all rising in,
Stagnant minds in flowing times,
A dream sets in reality.

Thinking stops for but a while,
And then the faces come out to play,
Scary thoughts in savage minds,
Stop to think is left behind.

Walls are all out screaming things,
And sounds they do surround,
Mystifying, pondifying,
Slowness settles in.

Noises all are floating about,
Streams of color rise,
Darkness enters once again,
But colored streams survive.

Tunes are quiet,
Filling in,
But shapes are soon to follow,
Brilliant flowing streams survive.

Slower the night seems to get,
Darker, yet with time,

Learning to Hate the World

Flowing streams get brighter yet,
Flowing slower, slower, yet.

Walls they seem to shrink,
Still yelling words of fear,
Others in the tangled net,
Quivering with frightened fear.

The floor it holds its own terror,
Crawling under toes,
Fearful thoughts are shared,
Crawling, squirming, shivering.

Blacker than black,
Streams lighter than light,
Floating shapes around,
At every peep of a sound.

Nothing ever can compare,
Reality is not thought there,
Dreaming thou are not,
Seeing things not seen.

The room is now full of black,
But neon colors streak,
Beeping once again forms shapes,
In the closing in of walls.

Those walls are buzzing,
As they descend further in,
Enclosing in the victim,
With a buzzing, humming, grin.

Feelings are not even thought,
Or even murmured in,
The hollow of the brain,
Now, itself, closing in.

A Journey Down the Wide Road

The fascination continues in,
Brighter in the dark,
Colors moving faster,
The humming getting louder.

Small dots appear in blots,
As they progress out of the walls,
Closing in, they follow you,
Trying only to get in.

The night progresses later yet,
The party on the roll,
Then you sit gleaming,
Gleaming at the floor.

The insects just start piling up,
Crawling up your spin,
Tingling, Tickling,
As they climb.

They reach the highest heights,
And start cracking down their shell,
The crunching is too hard to bear,
And shapes come even from there.

In desire to leave the ground,
And the creatures on the mound,
One is set up to level,
Only sink into the bevel.

The sand in the darkened cave,
Pulls you down to into,
Who knows where,
But only those who stay will know.

The terror is building high,

Learning to Hate the World

The shapes are floating round,
The walls are humming,
With that evil buzzing sound.

Nowhere to go, but inside,
And so you hide,
Under the blacker dome,
Seeking shelter from unknown.

The sounds that do surround,
Fill the crevices of your shelter,
With the brilliant color,
And walls are getting louder.

Fear is building up as high,
As the black dome topping the sky,
Filling in your mind,
With the hint of psychosis.

Fearing all who come your way,
You run to stay away,
But running does no good,
You are encompassed all around.

By the buzzing of the wall sounds,
Looping of the streams,
Floating of the shapes,
Never can escape...
Even when your done...with hit - #21.

I Hate Feeling So Good

High school is a complicated time. Part of those complications surround our emerging sexuality. In my case, the years of being used for other people's pleasure added to the conflict as I was torn between pain and pleasure. I generally hated my past sexual interactions but my body grew into yelling for it. My habits interfered, and I found myself caught between what I hated, but what I desired[1].

The still photos and video pornography I had collected in middle school remained of little interest to me as I matured. I may have even recorded over the tape in favor of some other program. The abuse died off around this time but I was still somewhat addicted to self-stimulation, keeping my heart bound up in conflict.

In ninth grade, like many boys, I became interested in girls. I sought out a relationship purely for the physical experimentation. Shannon, likewise, experimented with many guys, and our paths crossed for about a month of "relationship" though at the beginning of the year we also experienced a little "friends with bennies."

We sat together on the bus on the long trip back from a band competition at Saint Mary's. The journey back to Edinboro was long, and we got talking about kissing among other things which occur between two bored freshmen late into the evening.

"Have you ever kissed a girl?" She asked.

---

[1] Romans 7:15

"No," I sheepishly replied.

"Do you want to?"

Did a girl really have to ask such a question of a hormonally challenged high school boy? So that night on the bus, we allowed anything above the belt. I finished the night by answering "Yes" to the question about kissing a girl.

Shannon experimented with various guys, dating each one for only about a month. Nearing my 15th birthday, she asked me to go out with her. During my time in her rotation she made it to my house a few times. Wouldn't you know it, every time she did, Mom had planned to weed the garden right outside my bedroom window! Nevertheless, we were not stopped from anatomical exploration and we proceeded to do things kids should be ashamed to do with their mother outside the bedroom window.

Marching Band's greatest benefit was the biannual trip to a famous amusement park down south. The band participated in a parade down the main street of the park, and for our travels, we received three days to visit the park with our friends. The bus ride into the deep south lasted twenty-four hours, and I sat with Shannon for the daytime portion of the ride. Despite her mom sitting in the seat directly behind us, we continued our high school course in cross-gender anatomical studies.

After hours the boys and girls had to split up to sleep, but we sneaked back together after the chaperons dozed off. We also spent a day together in the park, but we parted ways as a couple and she went off to date another guy. I was free from relationship responsibilities and I returned to the empty pleasures in myself.

Leaving girls behind, I dove into movies and music as the distraction and release. Bob knew a lot about movies, so when I met him in the summer after my ninth-grade year. I was attracted to him for the movie recommendations. It turned out, however, that Bob resembled the boy in the neighborhood more than he did Larry.

The key difference is Bob was old enough to know that the things he wanted to do were wrong, while the neighborhood kid was acting on the same confusing ideas plaguing my own mind

Using my interest in movies, Bob gave me films to watch to "give me a wider perspective." In the 1990s Bob was gay, but since such a lifestyle was not in vogue, he would often say, "I'm not 'gay', I'm 'undefined.'" But this gay man did his best to coerce me into his lifestyle, and movies are a great propaganda tool.

Bob gave me *The Crying Game* to watch. The hero of the film meets up with a lady and forms a relationship. As they got together for intimate relations, he discovers she is really a cross-dresser. The point of the film is to build up love and then ask rhetorically how genitalia has anything to do with these ultimate feelings. The film represented a full-frontal assault on what is now called the "hetero-normative mindset." That was a calm film compared to the others he gave me including *The Genesis Children* and *For a Lost Soldier*. In retrospect, he was interested in coercing a change in my worldview, not being a friend.

I developed periods of lucidity when my life's conflict subsided, resulting in throwing Bob to the back burner of my life. These times came near the end of my tenth-grade year when I developed a love for academic studies. Also during these times Jake and I had forged our strongest friendship, and I was able to reconnect with Michael. This is the same summer my brother moved out and Mom and I were probably in the lowest level of conflict we had ever had. We were even turning into friends.

The start of my eleventh-grade year resumed conflict, mostly from moving in with William, having no where to go for hours after school, and Jake's visits declining. In these times, Bob opened the door to more visits and sprung his trap mixing his poisoned ideas with my personal conflict.

He made his move to have his way with me, more slyly than the neighbor kid. I was humiliated again. I thought my new-found knowledge would give me strength to fight off his ideas but I failed. My opinion of myself waned as I became weak to control my desires, and I hated every moment of his actions. Still, I kept a good face on it. He would only have his way with me in times of my weakness until I finally saw the devil he was. After I cut off contact with him he likely made his way with other troubled teenagers, and I know at least one kid he started talking to after I left him behind.

I learned about Bob's patterns by watching his interactions. I first noticed that he was not really interested in me as a friend when he never watched any of the movies I recommended, though I watched nearly everything he sent my way. He also let me borrow his book on herbs and when I bought a new copy for myself, he asked me to give him the new one rather than getting his own copy back (in the exact condition he lent it to me). Further, Bob tended to call me to come over late at night, and would try to convince me even through a "no". But if I ever called him he was too busy to hang out. Even one time I needed to talk to someone he ignored my request. Those observations led to the end of our "enemyship."

I had a single encounter with a man who showed me that Bob was not unique in his approach. I met this guy at a consignment shop where I sold herbs. On this day he had set up a table to perform Tarot card readings, and he struck up a conversation. He seemed to be an interesting person, so we exchanged phone numbers.

On one rainy, summer night, Bob had called (after 9:00 of course) and I used the excuse that I did not want to drive in the rain so I couldn't come over. He finally accepted my answer like a puppy with his tail between his legs.

This new guy called about half an hour later, and I used the same excuse. Unlike Bob, he had a car and offered to drive. I reluctantly agreed to come over for a while, "but not too long." His jeep pulled into the driveway and we returned to his apartment. He lived with a roommate who was away this weekend.

I didn't realize it at the time, but he was also gay. It became clear why he wanted me to come over. I was trying to be nice when I told him I was not interested in that lifestyle, but I have no problems with it otherwise, so we can still hang out. He offered me beer, which I rejected for a coke instead, and we sat down to watch a movie.

Sometime during the movie I fell asleep, and I woke up to find this gay man molesting me. I told him off and gathered my belongings for the walk home. He offered to drive me, but I lost all trust in this guy, so not only did I walk, but I took the lonely path through the cemetery and along the lake so he couldn't find me on the road should he have looked. I never saw him again after that.

My high school years started with confusing abuse, pornography, and self-stimulation but it ended with two gay guys trying to pleasure themselves off me; one whom wanted to indoctrinate me into his lifestyle. Yes, I think my adolescence may have been more sexually confusing than most of my peers, but it also gave me plenty more reasons to hate the world.

Ashes to Ashes, Dust to Dust

June 25, 1995

I saw the darkness
I saw the light
Now it is dull
And nothing remains
From either world
Ashes to ashes
Dust to dust
My dreams were strong
I remember them clear
I now remember nothing
But my dreams have faded
Ashes to ashes
Dust to dust
I had a friend
And we promised to the end
Never would we be severed
But in the end
Even he was gone
Ashes to ashes
Dust to dust
I started to hate
And I saw people to hate
I grew angered
For no true reason
Or did it emerge from
The group we were in
Ashes to ashes
Dust to dust

I Hate Feeling So Good

It came out of me
I am now glad
That part has left me
And I shall never be sad
Ashes to ashes
Dust to dust
The sadness came
And down I went
Further and further
Down the path of fear
Will it ever fade?
Ashes to ashes
Dust to dust
It has faded
A new friend is here
I now know not
Ever to promise...
But I did
Ashes to ashes?
Dust to dust?
I know now not
if it shall end???

Demons

Ashes to Ashes Dust to Dust 3

August 28, 1997

Each touch a tranquil sea
Yet phasing with hostility
Demon 2 wished the night
The happenings were all it's sight
I knew once before of the hideous race
I saw only after into a horrible face
It conquered my thoughts
My very do's, and do not's

A Journey Down the Wide Road

I saw the pattern in repetition
And my mind did set for some petition
I knew the fate of further
But the night I did not murder
I felt control of many men
And stated bluntly like paper and pen
A while longer the demon 2 talked
Up in a pace I turned and walked
The demon 2 knew it was in control
No votes on the matter, there was no poll
Continuing on after the hour
Turning the night rather sour
Control it gained faster on me
I would just have to wait and see
Once before, demon 1 got me
Why demon 2, i could not see?
I once knew to avoid the fate
I now know to avoid the late
Feelings flow, rage and hate
I had bitten the bait
I once knew to avoid the night
And company of demons in candle light
I wish I could erase a night in time
Calling the night, "wasted for mine"
Only when demon 2 looked near
I saw a baby in it's tear
A mask I knew for what it possessed
Ending in a night for molest
I looked into eyes, a revolution
For in my mind formed a solution
Never again be in demons' mind
Always run and hide behind
For demons possess a power
To let other thoughts be coward
Brain washed minds is where they live
And they need this power to take or give
But you rarely want a demons gift

I Hate Feeling So Good

For it is one that it may lift
I walked out of demon 2's life
Before my mind he did heist
Demon 1 I also avoid
Like a plague or a void
Contact still is kept not
A losing battle in I did fought
I now come out with victory
Because they will never touch me
Exchange of oblong smile
And after a while
A hint will form in it's mind
When will the demons read the sign?

Who Needs Your Useless God

People often seek power, and as their life spins out of control, they grasp at straws for whatever they can possibly hold on to. That defined my life at the end of my eighth-grade year. My discussions with Mindy gave me food for thought as I pondered the spiritual side of life. I began studying a basic primer on magick from a book in our school library. The college library had more advanced works, so I spent a lot of time there reading, studying, and transcribing the lessons into notebooks.

Magick was written with a rune language, converting the common tongue of the wizard into a coded alphabet. I dedicated myself to learn the runes until I could read the script with ease. The transcribed notes, spells, and methods were coded into the rune language, so I was the only person I knew who could read my notebooks.

In addition to the spells, magick required artifacts. A wand of sorts, special robes for the exclusive purpose of practicing the art, and candles were the basic equipment. Various spells required other materials. Perhaps a silver coin for financial gain or the hairs of someone who might be at the other end of the incantations. My little hidden bag of trinkets became a hiding place for my artifacts; the boyhood treasures slowly morphed into the secrets of a teenager.

In my studies I learned the difference between white and black magick. The difference is not in the spells being cast or the methodology, but the intention of the mediator. Karma might be a good word here. If the intention behind my art is to better my or another's life, it is by definition white magick. If I intend harm to my enemy, it is black. One must also always be cautious, for our fortunes might become another's misfortune. I learned to tread carefully down the path of the magical arts, and even the white spells I sought to cast were practiced with caution.

I had a deep-seated root of morality for reasons I couldn't understand[1], and this led me to only practice white magick. As my peers learned about my dabbling, they commissioned love spells for their teenage flirtations. I also had success in a spell for financial luck.

I performed my arts and carried the silver coin as the spell required. Robert and I walked through town the day of my spell's duration and found twenty dollars to split between ourselves. Later we visited the bookstore looking for a particular *Dungeons & Dragons* book. While staring in dismay that the book wasn't in stock, the owner came by and placed a used copy right on the shelf in front of me; the price was less than my cut of the twenty dollars. I had experienced financial luck indeed.

I grew stronger and more arrogant in my practice. But my experimenting with magick came to an end in the summer after my ninth grade year. Grandma became ill with lung cancer and deteriorated rapidly. A week after my final visit with her, Mom was staying there, and I received the call that she would probably not last the day. I immediately performed my rituals for strength and survival. I lit candles meant to stay lit until her body was overcome by healing, but I failed. She passed away as the doctors predicted. I was humbled with the knowledge that I was not able to prevent death.

---

1 Jeremiah 31:33

I didn't instantly destroy my artifacts, but like a kid who neglects his old favorite toys for new ones, I drifted on to other spiritual concerns mostly forgetting about the magical arts. I had other, more powerful pursuits to examine anyway. Those pursuits looked for the "gods" within all of us.

My first brush with this spiritual side of life occurred at Robert's house one night. Our little rag-tag outcast group stayed at his house for the night. We played a game called "Into Hell." The instructions were merely controlled meditation: the person about to go down would lay comfortably while the person leading him into Hell would count from ninety-nine to one as the traveler focused on walking down stairs. Once he reached the bottom, he stood at a door. Opening the door was opening the mind to Hell, or maybe a dungeon. He would describe what he saw as he traveled in his mind through the dark visions. We knew something dragged us around to these places.

On my second turn for the night, I said I wanted to go up to Heaven to prove that there is no God. Robert counted up to ninety-nine instead of down to one. I ascended the stairs, and as I proceeded upward, the vision in my mind grew bright even though the lights in Robert's room were all turned off.

I opened the door at the top step to a city in clouds. I saw happy people, but it was apparent they did not see me. As hard as I tried, I couldn't move. Stuck, I watched the visions before me for only a few minutes before being confronted with a face. I didn't recognize the man, but I felt this could be the "God" I stood denying. I knew I was not welcome in this place and instantly I jolted awake. The dark room suddenly replaced the bright clouds and I lie awake next to three friends who meddled with spiritual forces that none of us understood.

Spiritual encounters were not unusual at Robert's house. A few years prior during the large camp out, we played with an old Ouija board. This wasn't your modern Milton-Bradly special; the board was solid wood with letters etched into the surface with fire. We used the board to talk to the spirit world. One boy took particular sensitivity to the board and used it more than any of us. Before long, we noticed his face started to turn a red color and he grew irritated as the night wore on. A few times he yelled at us in a deeper, raspy, growling voice certainly not belonging to a prepubescent eleven-year-old. We were awed by the power of the board. That event stayed with us while we dabbled more.

With the thoughts of the spiritual world in my mind and having abandoned magick after grandma died, I went spiritually silent for a period of time. I rejected any notion of God, even rejecting him publicly before church-going kids in the neighborhood. Jake and I were both against drugs and were very moral for the most part, and this led us to be trusted to play tag, hide-and-seek, and other outdoor games with the kids in the neighborhood. It was a moment of reflection to the times we played such games on the block in Meadville.

One day, the topic of God arose while I was in the garage talking to the kids across the street from my house. They attended Sunday school regularly and talked about their belief in God. I replied that there is no God. To prove it I called for lightning bolts to strike me dead. No lighting came and I had my proof that God didn't exist. The kids tried to refute me but I didn't budge in my lack of belief in God.

By my eleventh-grade year when I started talking to Bob again, he tried to convince me to believe in Buddhism. I laughed at this prospect, particularly knowing enough about Buddhist thought to know their faith denies pleasure while seeking

Nirvana. The fact that Bob sought his own satisfaction to existential ends demonstrated his attraction to the "concept" of Buddhism, but he was clearly not a follower of the religion. His life's hypocrisy was not lost on me and I had the boldness to reject even his reliance on a deity.

My faith became New Age. This was a faith system that depended not on a God or a system, but on the power within us. New Age is brought on by discipline and work. The fruit of New Age is for the practician to acquire the power to control his own life and emotions. I found New Age thought by studying deeper into natural medicines and herbology.

My books on natural medicines preached the benefits of Yoga and meditation. Studying meditation further led me to hypnosis and the ability to place myself into a hypnotic, controlled meditation. Once I was able to attain control of my mind through meditation, I could use the power of suggestion to make myself perfect. The fruits started bearing themselves as I used this art to learn how to study, gain more knowledge, and overcome my academic deficiencies.

Hypnosis and meditation, like magick, work to a point. I identified weaknesses in myself and "suggested" them away. I learned new study habits and how to control my emotions when tested. My New Age practice showed me ways to deal with the immoralities and injustices the world had to offer. I finished high school in control of my emotions, pushing "immoral" people away to protect myself from their attacks on me. I learned how to learn, how to better myself, and I did it all without anyone's useless God.

Interlude: The Hound of Heaven

> I fled Him, down the nights and down the days;
> I fled Him, down the arches of the years;
> I fled Him, down the labyrinthine ways;
> Of my own mind; and in the mist of tears;
> I hid from Him, and under running laughter.
> ...
> I am He Whom thou seekest!
> Thou dravest love from thee, who dravest Me.
> - *Francis Thompson*

During my concluding days in middle school I faded into a deep sea of personal depression. I looked for ways out, though I knew drugs were not the ticket[1]. Could I find my path to sanity in education or New Age thought?

I grasped for personal dominance, and each time I received a fistful of empty power. It seemed each grasp showed me only a shadow of what was missing, but the joy faded with the morning dew. Maybe I just needed a good friend (one in my own school district) who was not interested in drugs.

I hated the world; it had nothing to offer me save pain and abuse. God, and even life, were both meaningless. As my hatred for the world grew strong, someone worked behind the scenes. He bent the strings of this world to His will and set invisible plans in motion[2].

---

1 Ecclesiastes 10:17
2 Romans 8:28

Interlude: The Hound of Heaven

After we arrived in Florida on the marching band trip I spent the day at the park with Shannon. It was exhausting; more so than staying up all night exploring human anatomy. Since Shannon wanted to spend the day with her friends, we mutually went off in our own direction for the third day. That meant I wandered the grand American amusement park alone, and I enjoyed my personal space.

"Hey! You're from General McLane, right?"

I turned around to see a high school-aged kid I hadn't seen before.

"Yeah," I replied. I truly didn't recognize him.

"Want to walk around for a bit?"

He was alone, like me, and seemed harmless enough.

"I'm Tom," I told him.

Remy had moved into town earlier that year. He had joined marching band playing the French horn. Like me, he was a loner, and he often found himself the brunt of schoolyard jokes. He had moved in from just south of where my grandma lived so we had a few things in common. He turned out to be a really good guy to hang around with since our personalities were very compatible. We spent the rest of the day in the park together seeing the sights.

Remy's dad had moved into town to accept the pastorate of one of the local churches and Remy generally fell in line with the teaching of his pastor-dad. He invited me to church, but I rejected the offers. I knew all about God, and I didn't want to consider what religion might offer. Remy was perfectly fine being a friend without sharing excessively about God, so we carried on a friendship through movies, *Dungeons & Dragons*

Interlude: The Hound of Heaven

(his parents didn't seem to see the game as evil as many religious people did), and later, *Magic: The Gathering*.

Remy introduced me to Mike, who had just started middle school. It was a little odd for a ninth-grader to hang out with a fifth-grader but we shared an interest in several video games, and for some reason his parents liked me. Mike's parents also raised him as a Christian and he also invited me to church. Once again I wasn't interested in talking about God.

Mike, like Remy, was very patient and understanding that I didn't want to go to church. They both happily maintained a friendship with me even if discussions about God were off the table. And any time they tried to talk about God I outmatched them intellectually, so I won the debate and changed the subject.

Remy graduated a year before me and rather than going off to college, he joined a traveling Christian drama ministry to act out the Gospel to the whole world. Mike and I remained good friends even after I had moved to Saegertown. Sometimes I stopped by his house or he might occasionally come over to my house for the weekend. Of course William was pretty hard on him, perceiving him as a little kid.

After I "woke up" in my tenth-grade year of high school, my Biology teacher, Mr. Hersh, saw a change in my demeanor. He kept an eye on what I was doing in high school and while I bumped into him in the hall a few times and had pleasant conversation with him, I really only talked to him again in my senior year.

Because I was supposed to skip my last year in high school, they were not expecting me to show up, but when I did, the guidance counselor scrambled to fit my single required elective into a whole academic year. I approached Mr. Hersh

Interlude: The Hound of Heaven

with the idea of being a teacher's assistant and he gladly accepted help with a physics course. For the next quarter he suggested that we do an independent study on something dealing with plants. I accepted a plan of action studying Bonsai trees.

One day when we were merely waiting for a tree to grow he asked another question.

"Are you a Christian?"

Oh no, here we go again, I thought.

"No. I don't see a need for God," I told him, "I study meditation and hypnosis that helps strengthen my mind."

"I thought since you started taking studies seriously and cut your hair you might have changed other things, too."

"No. I started a job in a restaurant, and they asked me to cut my hair for the job," I replied.

Mr. Hersh moved the conversation back onto God. I didn't really want to talk about God, but I was fascinated by any adult who took an interest in me without wanting to abuse me at the same time. Something about him seemed closer to Larry than Bob in the way Mr. Hersh talked to me.

"Do you want to talk about these things? I think I can clear up some misconceptions you might have about God," he offered.

"I don't mind talking about it, but don't expect anything," I said rather arrogantly.

Mr. Hersh showed some basic ideas about what he believed but suggested we might talk more after school one day. That was fine by me. I welcomed any excuse to get out of the house.

Interlude: The Hound of Heaven

We still lived in Saegertown (this was right before we moved to the cottage in Edinboro) and as it turned out Mr. Hersh also lived in Saegertown, only about two miles from the house from hell. He stopped by one day, and we took a drive out to some property we owned further up the road.

He told me more about his God and gave me the first Bible I ever owned along with a few other books written about worldviews and Christians. We talked a little more about these things at school and Mr. Hersh was the first person I ever encountered who believed in God *and* had logical answers to real questions. He had the academic prowess to counter my objections, but in the end I rejected his ideas about God. About this time life spun out of control again causing us to leave Saegertown, and I got an after school job, so I never met up with Mr. Hersh after school during the year.

I finished high school and moved on to college. During orientation week I learned about job opportunities in the college planetarium. Because I loved walking at night and desired to learn more about the stars, I stopped in for a tour of the planetarium. The director, Dr. Daniels, was a funny and nice, and often goofy professor. I liked him a lot and wanted to work at the planetarium, but for reasons Solomon couldn't figure out, the school determined that me, a poor kid from a single-parent home, was not qualified to work on campus. Out of character for me, I volunteered to work at the planetarium for free.

One night after a public showing of the night sky I stayed on for a while and Dr. Daniels asked me if I knew God.

Uggg, I thought again. *Where do these Jesus freaks keep coming from?*

"No. I don't see a point in God," I told him.

Interlude: The Hound of Heaven

Dr. Daniels's approach was different from that of the other people I had met. Remy and Mike had tried to defend God to me, and they failed. Mr. Hersh had given me actual answers, but I still rejected. Dr. Daniels asked a lot of questions about why I didn't have a need for God. His questions were neither arrogant nor belittling, but very serious. He was interested in finding out what I believed. I explained my study of meditation and hypnosis and how they gave me control over my thoughts and emotions. I didn't have a reason to seek God; I was a god unto myself.

He kept the door open to talk about God anytime and he had some Bible tracts lying around that I could read if I wanted to, but I didn't take much interest in such myths. I told him that I talked a lot about God with my teacher in high school but I didn't believe in it all.

"Mr. Hersh?" he asked.

"How did you know?" I replied.

"Oh, I know him. He is the biology teacher where you graduated."

I was a bit stunned by this proposition. I talked a lot about God with my teacher in high school, and now, out of character with myself, was volunteering with another Jesus Freak and those two knew each other!

First, God is softening me up with two steadfast young Christians who couldn't give me answers but could not be rattled from their faith. And they were the nicest kids I knew. Then I talk about God with a teacher who is my academic superior. He could answer my questions, but still I rejected God. Finally, he sends me to a friend of the teacher who demonstrates the most real love I have ever seen a man demonstrate. This is beyond mere coincidence; this is conspiracy!

God himself sent sowers to throw some seeds into my mind. He wanted to show me that all those fake Christians of the past were not who He really is. But I wasn't yet ready to be broken. That would come later by His hand. I continued rejecting all these offers to "meet God."

I was being pursued, but I was not ready to be caught. The hunt was on.

Sin's Stronghold

For what I am doing, I do not understand; for I am not practicing what I would like to do, but I am doing the very thing I hate.
Romans 7:15

Losing All Respect

For a biochemistry student, college is hard. On the first day of biology 101, the professor entered the classroom with a bold proclamation.

"There are thirty-five students in here right now. At the end of the semester, only twenty will be left, and only half of those will pass."

This guy had prophetic blood in his veins. On the last day of class I counted the nineteen remaining students. The grapevine told me that only eight of us had passed the course. I found myself in that group, and we trotted on to harder courses among the shattered dreams of our fallen comrades.

Unlike high school, however, I had to try. I didn't have any more days of showing up to class and studying other materials instead of focusing on what the professor taught. Despite the trials and required study, I still managed to land on the Dean's list with my moderate first semester load of biology, pre-calculus, English 101, and poetry.

During this first semester at college we gave up our cottage in Edinboro and returned to the house in Saegertown with William. Life in the country still lacked luster, but now I had a car, a full time college course load, and a job. All taken together, I had enough things to keep me from being at the house, and on the days I didn't work, the library and college buildings provided ample spaces to "live" while I studied and completed assignments.

My need to study amplified in my second semester. Though I put forth a lot of studying, I still failed my first chemistry exam. I felt prepared and even felt that I had done well, but clearly I didn't. I needed to change something, so I took a more immersive approach. I purchased extra books and tools, and worked so hard that I eventually finished the class in the top seat. But this meant twice as much studying as I initially planned, and this was on top of four other classes.

The workload of a serious college student is lost on blue-collar workers, and this led to conflicts in not being able to meet unreasonable demands on my time. William still insisted on his lawn being mowed exactly on Saturday, but I often worked an eight-hour shift on Saturday in addition to lab reports and computer programs that were required on Monday mornings. A Friday lawn-mowing was still not an option, so I learned to vanish before anyone woke up on Saturday and I generally stayed away until Sunday morning when I would get to the lawn very early. This appeased the "gods" but still created a rocky relationship. At least the task of lawn mowing faded into the winter by the end of the first semester.

Early into my second semester in college while I struggled to pass chemistry, every semblance of decency at home came crashing down. On the first weekend in February I had a lot of homework. This was not merely studying, but a chemistry lab, a computer program, a set of calculus problems, and more odds and ends of the generic general education courses we were forced to endure.

I worked straight through that Saturday finishing about half of my work, but I was scheduled to start my closing shift at the restaurant at 5:00. I asked to skip my break so I would be done as soon as the doors closed at 1:00 AM. My plan went off without a hitch as far as the front of the restaurant was concerned. But in the back, Steve was on shift. He was the slowest and most incompetent worker that ever graced the store in my two years working there. When the doors locked, the front of the restaurant was the epitome of clean. Every table shined, every salt and pepper dispenser neatly stood ready like a picture-perfect line of soldiers.

To contrast the front perfection, the back of the store looked like a war zone. The pre-close tasks, usually completed by 8:00, had not yet been started. I had no idea what Steve was doing all night; we really were not all that busy. But the policy states that all employees have to leave at the same time, so I growled to my self in seething anger and started doing anything I could that would not interfere with the sink that was now full of fryer filters.

Steve cut himself and proceeded to bleed all over the sinks. His blood was a deterrent for me to clean anything in that area, so I tackled the hood, wiped down the counters, organized and stocked the soda syrups...all while Steve stood there for an hour holding a broom in his hand, but failing to sweep up the piles of sesame seeds that accumulated on the floor. I finally told the manager to make him clean up his blood and get out of the store. I finished cleaning the rest of the place by myself and clocked out 6:30am – a thirteen-hour shift without a break. I made it home after sunrise.

Two hours of sleep later, the tyrant yelled to get up. No compromise, no discussion. He wanted to get a load of wood from the neighbors house, and in his uncompromising mind, it had to be done now. I yelled for an hour reprieve, but that was not happening. We went over to get the wood when he demanded why I was so lazy and didn't want to help get wood.

Bearing my answer to a fool, I attempted to explain my night, but it was all excuses to his one-mind ways. He decided to show his dominance, so he punched me in the face and threw me into the pile of wood.

I pulled myself from the pile and ran into the house. This was a guy with guns who had threatened me several times before, so I chose to leave. I grabbed the school books, a few days of clothes, and a few other odds and ends and ran out to my car to escape. I fled the driveway without thinking about where to go. Perhaps out of instinct I arrived at Sally's house where I could take a shower and finish the rest of my homework assignments. While I was there, Mom called to tell Sally how I attacked William. Sally told her that was simply not true. She knew what kind of tyrant William was, and she had the courage to tell my mother that her story wasn't true. Even still, Mom tried to tell that story to everyone she knew, though all her friends rejected her allegations.

I met with Mom a week later and tried to tell her that I am happy to help out with things, but I have to have notice and schedule it in. I also need flexibility. I attempted to show her what a full time college load looked like, but while I was trying to do that, she was trying to look through my papers to see my grades! I was livid. At this meeting after all her friends told her that I would never attack William, she still never sought to set the record straight. I lost all my respect for my mother that day.

February's Dream
May 19, 1998

A pressing hand upon my land
Creates pressure high and high
Upon the light of a thousand dreamers
I held my secrets high
Dreamers come and dreamers go
Most are shattered hope
Losing faith at difficult day.
The sky was blue, day was crisp
Spring was in the air.
Tomorrow will tell if it was dear.
Upon the land, a shadow cast, loving
Dreams for feed. Lowering sky's, eyes
Bulged wide, a mistake we'll never forget
Losing faith was all I had, shattered hope remained
Any one but I would take to the blade, support, no
More here. Forgetting then would be pain
I work now more and more. Harder tasks covered
At last, only ease is left for here
Forgetting past, murdered now, your future is just a blur,
What is left for you to see; I don't want it to be me.
The hardest task accomplished at last, "proud" of you
Will say. No thanks to you, your support is gone,
Respect will not return. You knew it once, a lesson you
Would never forget; love does make you blind.
Nothing you say in comparison to whom you wish to compare.
Once was first as always is, in every thing and day
Your analogy sucks, like your thoughts; do you know of a moral?
The first fist raised creates the rule, allows if I allow
Just as you; you stupid bitch, I thought you would know by now...

Sin's Stronghold

Within his presence, seconds expand...
Murder Me and you will pay. When your need is high.
Sit down in your rocking chair, Smoke some Marijuana.
Control your world as you wish. Rule her now again
Let her suffer, I will shatter you ALL...

Suicidal Tendencies

On the Sunday morning that William attacked me, I first headed to Sally's house. As the basecamp for our old battles with him, it somehow seemed right. From all the old conflict, she knew my story was the correct one. It matched all the traits she already knew from our previous flights from that house. I was able to spend the afternoon getting a shower and finishing the homework that was due the following morning.

Afterwards, I went to the restaurant to tell the supervisor that she can schedule me full time. Along with providing more income, this decrease the time I'd need to fill with being "elsewhere." I could easily figure out how to fit studying into the day. From the parking lot with my big cell phone, I started making calls. I reached out to Jake and asked about staying at his house for a while. His parents hated William and invited me to stay as long as I wanted, though I hated the feeling that I was using friends. Still, I chose to stay there for a few nights every week. Before heading out there, I called Michael. He wasn't able to do much from California, but at least I had someone to talk to for a while.

Jake's house was about as far from the college as the house in Saegertown, though from a different direction. I stayed on a couch in Jake's room – a detached garage converted into a nice bedroom that was just far enough from his parents to allow him to stay there while he figured out his life. They didn't expect payment but asked that I give Jake a ride to work on the mornings I was there. It actually worked out perfectly because his job was on the way to the college and I arrived at campus at exactly the right time to park in a good parking spot for the day. I used the car as base camp during the days to study, stage books for classes, and to just hang out when I had extra time.

I still felt uneasy about staying at Jake's house all the time, but I retrieved personal possessions from Saegertown to take to his house. I arrived on a Thursday afternoon, but unfortunately, Mother was at home. I marched into the house to my room, ignoring her all her pleas to talk all the way up the steps. I tore down the computer and stereo components (what teenager can live without that?) and packed the car full of electronics and other things that were important to me.

"Where are you going?" Mom asked.

"I'm leaving. That is all you need to know!" I barked back.

"I need to know where."

"Why?" I yelled.

"Because I'm your mother," she retorted.

I'm your mother?!? I thought to myself. *What mother lies about her husband attacking her child? What mother does not respond to pleas to do something about this tyrant?*

I kept quiet, finished packing the car, and left. Toni Braxton's *Unbreak My Heart* played on the car stereo as I pulled out of the driveway, still mostly uncertain about my future.

Once back at Jake's house that night, I set up the computer in his living room so I could do my Visual Basic computer programming assignments. Had it not been for that class, I might have just left the computer behind. As for the stereo, I set that up in Jake's room, and we listened to music on shuffle as we'd done in the good old days of our tenth-grade weekends.

For a week, I sometimes stayed on Jake's couch and other times I parked my car in the back lot of the Edinboro Mall. It was still February and sleeping in the northeast in a car that time of year isn't a comfortable prospect. Still, I captured the minimum sleep necessary to function, and spent the rest of my time either working or studying.

By the end of the week, Mother called and wanted to talk. We planned to meet at the Subway restaurant not far from campus. This was one of my regular study spots and the manager knew my order once I walked in the door. She had no problem with my commandeering a table for up to three hours every few days. It was my Switzerland to meet for our negotiations.

For this meeting, I dragged in all my college books and even the time cards from my job. I also showed the type of work I need to do and explained the average estimation of needing to study and prepare homework for about two extra hours for every hour in class. I reiterated that I am happy to help out at home, but I need advance notice to schedule things in, and I need flexibility for when I get to odd requests. These seemed to be non-negotiable with the tyrant. She asked me to come back, but I couldn't affirm that I would. I only said I would think about it.

The second week became more difficult. I spent only three nights at Jake's house, but still felt bad about using his parents house as my new de-facto home. I went over there only on days I had computer programming assignments to complete; at that time, many other reports were still completed by hand, so a computer was not such a necessity as today.

On the days I didn't stay at Jake's house, I parked in various places around Edinboro. Since I didn't have any overnight parking stickers, I didn't try parking on campus, but I closed the restaurant not far from the college, so often I would sleep in the car after work, then go in for breakfast the following morning to chat with my work friends. Other nights, the mall parking allowed me a few hours of sleep.

The third week wore down on me. My pride prevented me from wanting to stay at Jake's, though his parents kept affirming I could stay as long as I needed. The parking lots were cold, and I was feeling more lonely than I ever had. I drove by the house a few times, pondering if I should go back. I didn't feel ready, so I kept driving and went up a mile past the house to where a sportsmen's club had a little building with a small parking lot on the dirt road. I back into the spot and hopped into the back seat for another cold night of sleep.

This back and forth with parking the car in cold lots and sometimes staying at Jake's wore me down. One night I thought I might just pull into the driveway and go back "home," but again, I was not able to turn in. I took the spot up at the sportsmen's club again. I hopped out of the car to look over the embankment that the parking lot sat upon. The drop down the sheer cliff to the railway tracks below was about seventy-five feet. The rail line was on a narrow flat, wide enough for the double tracks and then took another twenty feet to the river below. I walked those tracks many times as a teenager. I looked up that cliff that I now gazed down. It was far enough.

I got back into the car and pondered the challenges of the recent months. I had few friends, no real family, and nothing but a hard life. The bitter cold of the February night bit my extremities, so I turned on the car for some heat. I thought about that cliff behind me. One quick thrust of the gas and I could be descending rapidly onto the tracks below. Would the car explode or just crumble into pieces? Did I stare at certain death, or was there a risk of mere injury. I shifted the car into reverse with the plans of slamming the gas, sending the car over the embankment. It was too easy until two thoughts ran through my mind.

My first thought was one of probabilities. What was the chance of a fiery explosion verses my old land yacht withstanding just enough impact to keep me but an inch from death. If my plan was not complete; if I did not have a 100% chance of ending it all, the probabilities were not in my favor. If I was injured, or merely lost the car, I would then be dependent on the very people I sought to escape.

Second, I wasn't a pushover. My years of coping with struggles in life strengthened my resolve rather than weakened it. If I cast myself over this cliff, it was a sign of resignation that William had won. The tyrant didn't pilot my ship's destiny; he had merely commandeered it for a period of time. I needed to set my own plan back in motion to regain my destiny. And it was not worth killing myself over a fool such as him.

I shifted the car back into park and sat, formulating a plan in my mind. The temperature of the car was again comfortable, so I turned it off and hopped into the back seat and wrapped blankets tight around myself. I echoed my plan in my mind. *Make it through college, get a good job, and leave this miserable excuse for a family completely in my past.*

Paranoid in the Upper Room

When I awoke in the morning, the frost-coated car windows were reminiscent of some steampunk Norman Rockwell scene. The biting cold awakened me just as the sun was fully illuminating the sky, but it had not yet peaked over the treeline. I jumped over the seat to turn the car on, then exited the vehicle to start scraping the windows. It was odd being a mile from the house, but not staying there. It was freeing in a way.

I sat in the car contemplating the prior night. I had chosen not to go over the cliff. I had chosen a new plan, an academic one. But I needed help. I drove to campus early that morning, arriving just as the commuter lots started allowing cars to park for the day. I walked into Dr. Daniels' office, though I'm not sure why. Maybe it was because he demonstrated a caring for people that I hadn't experienced since my high school biology teacher.

"Do you have a minute?" I asked.

"Sure," he said, placing his pen on a stack of to-be graded exams.

I started unfolding the details of my horrible evening and how I wanted to drive off the cliff. When I told him about the situation with William and the lack of any family support, he stopped me.

"I can't really relate to family problems," he started, "I had wonderful parents and a great home...but my wife experienced the things you have. Hang on."

He stopped talking and grabbed the phone. He spoke softly with the woman on the other end of the line. It was a way I had never seen men talk to their wives; an alien conversation endured, then he hung up the phone.

"Can you come to my house for lunch?" Dr. Daniels asked.

I met him at his office an hour later and we walked a few blocks off campus to where he lived. Between bites of a sandwich, Mrs. Daniels asked me a series of questions about my home life. I had never heard of a "dysfunctional family" before, so she explained what it meant. A few parts of my psychology course came to mind and I understood a little more about the things I was dealing with. Of course, knowing what we are dealing with is not the same as knowing what to do in such a situation, so I had more questions.

"What can I do about all this?"

"Give your life to Jesus," Dr. Daniels said.

"I know about 'God' but that stuff isn't for me," I answered.

Mrs. Daniels cut in, "If you don't want to give it to Jesus, the best you can do is realize the dangers present in your family and build a wall around yourself to keep yourself safe."

Her advice became part of my plan. I didn't need any useless Jesus in my life. Instead, I needed to avoid the crazy people in my house at all costs. That meant occasionally sleeping in my car at work, staying up really late at the library, and figuring out how to avoid sub-human contact at the house when I had to go there. This was the first cornerstone of my newly-formed plan.

Second, I desired the highest academic standards possible. I would do anything it took to keep the highest possible grades, but I also knew I needed to stay in the good graces of my professors. Good grades are not what makes a good student. Dedication, serious study habits, and good communication with the professors are the things that makes a good student. I started pridefully despising the students who didn't want to study. I also hated those who thought college was a time to play and party – to extend the immaturity of high school. I was here to learn, and if you were not interested in that, stay out of my way.

Finally, my plan saw money as a resource that would help me achieve my goals. Since the college had said I couldn't have a job on campus, I asked the restaurant to schedule me for as many hours as they wanted. This meant I was making more money and more of my time could be spent out of the house. Despite an increase in scheduled work, I still fit in my studies by excluding everything from my life that wasn't directly related to working or college. This crowded out all my old hobbies, all the old friends, and all the old places. I turned into a work horse, but one with an eye toward the future.

House-life during this period became something I despised. I held myself always on guard against the next attack, but I figured out how to live in a house with two other people and never see them at all. My plan started with staying at the library studying until they closed at midnight. I headed back to the house, and approached the door in an odd zigzag pattern so as to not trip any of the motion sensor lights, which could awake someone. I moved through the house like a ghost, slipping into my bedroom and sliding a big rock in front of the door to secure it. I set a small alarm on my watch and laid down on a pad set on the floor, clutching a knife while I slept.

Sin's Stronghold

My morning routine was static for the rest of the semester. The alarm awoke me at the same time William got up. I listened intently for all the regular sounds he made. I heard the distinct creaks his heavy body made while going down the stairs. The door to his room with his private shower made a distinct slide and shut. While he showered, I was free to make a little noise while I gathered the things I needed for the day ahead of me. I heard the distinct noises of his kitchen chair sliding into place while he lit his morning cigarette, always two strikes with the lighter...distinct from Mother's three strikes. I smelled the air as the smoke rose to my upper bedroom and I listened in silence like a lion watching his prey from the edge of a field, crouching in the grass out of sight. Next I heard the heavy front glass door close shut and then from the driveway heard the car start. He always sat there for about three minutes before shifting the truck into reverse and backing out of the driveway. I watched the truck disappear down the road, and I knew I had only twenty minutes before Mother's alarm clock rang.

The next phase of my morning routine meant preparing to leave. My room was occupied territory, a bunker in enemy lands, so I didn't keep anything essential there. The most important necessities were kept in the car, meaning I only needed the clothes on my back and the book bag for my day. I stripped down and took clean clothes and the backpack to the bathroom and took the fastest showers I have before or since. Just enough to get clean, in and out, dry off, and throw the new clothes on. I never went back up stairs. I grabbed my bag and headed out the door, often hearing the initial buzz of Mother's alarm clock while silently closing the heavy glass door. I escaped silently to my car and drove to campus for the next day.

For the rest of the semester I kept this plan in full force. I learned what paranoia means. Every noise was cataloged, every scent was analyzed. I learned whom the morning cough belonged to, and I knew what every sound was to the finest detail. I had learned the skill of hypervigilence, and it served me well. I used these skills and my timing to live in that house from March until the end of the semester in May before I even saw William or Mother again.

Footsteps

May 24, 1998

Silence in the upper level
Listening...Paranoid
Footsteps walk the ground
Creating a crashing sound

Silence in the upper level
Listening...Paranoid
Hearing the ones below
But up still I stow

Silence in the upper level
Listening...Paranoid
Hearing sounds of long ago
Thinking from now to first snow

Silence in the upper level
Listening...Paranoid
Crying sounds, they filled my head
Wishing then instead

Silence in the upper level
Listening...Paranoid
Then or will please
But the present...please leave

I'm tired of the torment
Sick of the pain
Forget all the others
My mind is my game

Paranoid in the Upper Room

Sanity...I must keep
Sanction I do seek
Leave behind the scheme
At first chance, I will leave
I hope it won't take long
But I must live by song
Likely dream at last
I do enjoy the past
I look now toward the future
Still thinking of the past
Build off it I will
But seek down this hell
Destroy my pain, make it go
Please defy...I will cry
I wanted then forever
But will not happen.
I just want now to go far and fast away...

Pridefully Successful

After placing my plan into effect, I became academically unstoppable. I grew mistrustful of other people causing my social circle to shrink into a pencil point. I didn't care. I busied myself with studying or working. Occasionally I would help other people struggling with their homework at the tables in the chemistry department, but it was hardly because I liked anyone. I merely found this as a good way to find the holes in my own knowledge. Work, study, study, work; nothing else mattered for this season of my life.

By the end of my first semester when I was attacked, I slowly loosened up enough to be in the house when people were awake, though I would seclude myself in my room, only exiting at times I wouldn't encounter anyone. I could muster a "Hi" if I needed to. My lax time at the house precipitated from the unknown schedule in the summer. I wanted to prepare should I find myself in the House from Hell between semesters. A new schedule presented itself. I took a second job for the summer and somehow fit in two classes in between. For the first month, I opened one restaurant, left in time for class, sat through a four-hour lecture on intercultural communication, and then closed another restaurant. I would drive to the first place after the shift was over to sleep in the car waking up just in time to go to work again.

Not long after finishing my first summer course, I left one of the restaurants to work at a larger store in Erie, which paid an extra dollar an hour. My brother also worked at this store, and he lived nearby, so I had a new place to stay. It was during this time when we finally became friends, mostly because of a shared hatred for William. This situation meant I stayed mostly in Erie except for the times I opened the store in Edinboro or when I had class.

My brother still had his wild parties, but after high school, confirmed by Hank Williams Jr, all the rowdy friends started settling down. The few drinkers in the crowd enjoyed their boozes while most of them passed a bull around the circle in one direction while the Sony Playstation controller passed the opposite direction. I thought myself above these fools, but I quietly sat in the middle of their circle drinking knowledge from textbooks when it wasn't my turn on Soul Blade.

I designed my arrogance and attitude toward pushing people away. I didn't want to be bothered by the people whom I saw as beneath me. I showed respect for the professors because they had achieved more than I had academically. The respectability I showed to the teachers was part of my plan to not get derailed from my future needs by pleasure, parties, or distractions.

The following school year saw much the same pattern as the summer. I stayed at my brother's house over the weekends when I worked, and stayed at the library until it closed. I excelled in several classes, taking the top grade in nearly every course and curving our principles of chemistry class. I was at the peak of arrogance by the end of the semester and rolled into summer still working at the restaurant, also now working for the chemistry department, and taking a few classes to make sure I would be finished with all my coursework in time to graduate in four years – five was not an option.

Over the summer, however, home life took another turn for the worse. William stopped locking his dogs up in his room at night and they had the run of the house. Since William didn't like me, his dogs followed suit and would growl and snap at me when I walked by. This was not his mother's Chihuahua, but his very large Dobermans. I did the best I could at avoiding them, but on one summer morning as I prepared to go to my mythology course, his dog barked and snapped more. I lunged at the dog just enough for it to back up, giving me time to escape out the door. William ran out of the house and fired his shotgun into the air before pointing it at me. I hastily slammed on the gas throwing up dust and stones and charged out of the driveway, nearly rolling into the side of the embankment.

I made it to class a few minutes late, heart still beating from the adrenaline, and I was now expected to sit in a three-hour lecture on old religions. The boredom overcame me, and I was calm, but rattled again, by the end of the lecture. I left class and headed to the chemistry department for my daily dose of cleaning and organizing the department. My adviser saw my different countenance and asked what was wrong.

"My home life just sucks. I got chased out with a shotgun this morning."

That was not the answer Leslie had expected, but being a brilliant scientist with excellent people skills, she composed herself, "Why don't you just move out?"

That is a question I examined from every point of view. At one point I criss-crossed town and read all the papers for apartments and rooms, but being a full time college student and part-time baker at a restaurant, rent was out of reach, unless I wanted to start taking out loans to get by. I saw debt as a hindrance, so I didn't like that option. I figured that getting out on my own may cost me freedom in the future.

"I looked at every option, and I just can't afford it without seriously hurting my future," I paused enough for reflection, "I just deal with it as I can."

She had a hint of compassion in her eyes as she thought of solutions. She continued, "Hold on. I think I saw an email of interest this morning."

I sat down on the bench, admiring the Grateful Dead bear stickers dancing on the filing cabinet.

"Yes," she said, breaking the silence, "Today they put out a call for a new Scholar in Residence. It turns out the old one has to transfer to a new school and just found out."

"What's that?" I asked curiously.

"A live in tutor," she said, "We have a new program in the residence halls where we put all the science majors on the same floor. One of them is an upperclassman who can tutor students in the sciences. It comes with a free dorm room."

The position started in a month, so I just needed to keep safe for that long until I could have a place to live for the semester. I had all the requirements: Entering my junior year, had good grades, was on good terms with the professors. I only needed to get a few professors from different disciplines to endorse me. Leslie was the first, Dr. Daniels was the second, and I had a friend in the math department whom I talked to a lot on ICQ, so he became the third. By the end of the day, a representative from each science department had unanimously recommended me to the position, and within twenty-four hours of being chased away with the shotgun, I now had a safe place to live for my last two years of college.

Luck and coincidence pulled the strings in just the right way to get me both a job and a place to live for the last two years of college. This was the result of my plan: study hard and be in good graces with the professors. My own efforts brought my good fortune. I didn't need a god!

Who Are You, Dad?

I moved into the dorms suddenly. The letter I received said residence hall training started in the second week of August. If I were a wiser person, I would have realized this was move-in day, but since I was a commuter and never lived in college dorms, the concept of "move-in" slipped my mind. As always, I was on time for the meeting, but that was the day I received my keys. I was ecstatic to have a room to myself, and I moved a few odds and ends that were always in my car into the room, but I would need to make a drive back to the house to retrieve the rest of the things I needed. Mother was not happy to learn that I was moving onto campus that night without any notice. Such a sudden change caused her to make an attempt at some level of control, so without consulting me, she reached out to my biological father to tell him that I am working really hard to go to school and that he should pay some of the bills.

We really didn't need help, even though I decided not to take out any more loans the prior year. I hated debt and on the day mother forced me to sign the student loan papers was one of the largest fights we ever had. But being reasonably smart, I decided that I wouldn't show up in my fourth semester to sign my signatures to accept the money. State Universities were still pretty cheap back then, and I was able to pay seventy-five percent with my multiple jobs, leaving mom to help with the last thousand or so dollars a semester. It was not that hard to pay for school.

Nevertheless, Dad wrote back a long letter saying that if I needed help, I should ask for it myself. Still, his letter was the perfect bridge from the childhood absentee father to two adults looking to start some degree of friendship. He explained some things from the past that I had only guessed at. I learned it was him who asked Child Protective Services to check on us during the early days with Michael.

He explained the attempts he made at reaching out to us, but that mother made it difficult. I knew his letter was true. She always cut him down and discouraged any communication. Children usually need to be goaded into things like reaching out to people they don't see every day, but mother never took the time to do that. He always had the same phone number and address, but I had never received that information. His letter finally included how I could reach him, so I called him to meet for dinner.

We planned to meet at Ruby Tuesday down the road from the restaurant where I worked in Erie. I headed in, not even knowing what my dad looked like. He had arrived early and sat at the bar looking toward the door. After a moment, a strange, large man called to me from across the mostly-empty dining room. I am not sure he knew who I was either, but a single college-aged adult with a confused look must have been the tell-tale sign. I had the look of terror exhibited by a middle student on the first day of lunch. Once he called out my name I looked up and confirmed. We moved to a nearby booth. I noticed immediately that several of our mannerisms were similar. The way we talked, ate, and even occupied empty hands told of our genetic connection.

After a brief round of pleasantries, he changed the conversation to money. Probably because my mother told him he should be helping to pay for college, he came expecting that I would ask him to. But I wasn't interested in money at all. I was interested in meeting this perfect stranger who was so much like myself.

"I don't want your money," I said. It was true, partly from my pride in not wanting to ask for help, but partly because he was still a total stranger to me. I had not earned the right to his money. I continued, "I came here to meet you, not your wallet."

He was taken aback. He probably expected me to look for money in the same way mother had done so all through our life. He explained it all in his letter to me. He told about how she made it difficult for him to see us, but still demanded money at every turn. While he confessed he was not always able to provide it, he would eventually pay his due support. I think he expected the constant fight over money he had with mother to continue with me. I, on the other hand, was looking for relationship. I am not sure if he was ready for that, but we both promised to try.

We had a good dinner and promised to meet up on a regular basis to attempt to forge a relationship. My course load and work made it hard to find time, and his business kept him occupied. I cannot recall if we met up again for another year, though we did exchange emails, which was a novel technology in those days.

All in all, I learned over the years a bit more about Dad. We met up every once in a while when I would pass through town, but a deep relationship never launched. He was never really a "father" like Michael was, but maybe a bit more like an uncle: he would meet up once in a while, say some kind words, buy dinner, and then we wouldn't talk for another year or so. It was just an extension of my times first meeting him in college. I really wasn't looking for a father. I made it this far without one. I did not need a father on earth or one in heaven.

Father

August 4, 2001

Father made a mistake one day
That mother could not forgive
We went with mother far away
To far to go to live

Daddy had a dream in him
That I would never know
To get to know him, chances Oh so slim
Mother did a fine job being sure to show

How daddy went away from us
And how bad he really was
Mother kept him from us
Why? Just because

Through the years amplifies
feelings in your mind
Mother being mad at him justifies
Our denial of time

He lived at one address
All his life
While moving made my life a mess
While mother chasing perfect life

We never knew where he was
For mother was afraid
We would send a letter
Not to be afraid

But daddy knew how we were
And that was not so good

Who Are You, Dad?

For he sent help to be sure
We were treated as we should

But daddy could not hear
From his source how we were
And we were far away, not so near
But my time was just a blur

Mother fell into arms
For fear of life alone
It took three years to sound alarm
She packed us up and moved back home

Said daddy would be by
And then he had to cancel
I let out a sigh
I bet mother had to cancel

For now I know how he is
I understand a dream
I also know how mother is
She keeps no long dream

Times with a Temptress

Becoming a dorm rat changes the college experience, even when you don't intend it to. I wanted freedom from possible death, and a free dorm room solved such a problem. Commuting to the university gives freedoms that living on campus doesn't. For the first two years, I arrived in the morning, selecting my spot in the central commuter lot, and then using that as a staging ground to crisscross campus. The freedom included the ability to vanish for long periods of time. Sure, one could find my car, but where I was, could be anyone's guess.

Dorm life, on the other hand, means the staging ground has an address. The amenities meant it was more practical to spend time in the room than other places, so anyone could be more easily tracked down on a moment's notice. While I loved the freedom and safety living on campus provided, the "being found" part was disconcerting for someone who wanted to remain a ghost.

Enter Annie. We first met during the prior semester in general chemistry II. Being on top of the class meant students often sought out my help for problems and to study. I was mostly easy to find on chemistry days because the department had a majors-exclusive room and a lot of study tables in the hallway cubicles. She sought me out for help on some of the concepts we covered in class.

Annie was a returning student around forty years old. Her career up to now involved para-medicine, but she wanted to move up the ladder further, so she quit her job, sold her house, and used her funds to pay for college while working part time to meet the rest of her expenses. Returning students often struggle with science concepts, so she sought a lot of help, and we became as much of friends as I was interested in, which usually meant helping her when I felt like it. When the semester ended, I forgot all about her, like I had done with most of the people I met in my college years. This new semester, however, she came up to say hi at the end of our first day in organic chemistry.

I always scored high on three-dimensional concepts cognitive tests, so organic chemistry was a breeze for me. Like the course prior, I kept the highest (or nearly so) in this class and the two other courses I took at the same time: analytical and physical chemistry. While the department warned against taking that kind of course-load, I was able to manage it fine, and still kept up on top. Seeing that I didn't struggle with organic chemistry, Annie came for help again. We exchanged email addresses, and it turns out, she had quite a vile and sexual sense of humor. She was the type that filled your inbox with crude jokes – such jokes I often really enjoyed.

While I kept my distance from most people, including Annie, she seemed to develop a fascination with me. Sometimes I got the feeling that she asked for help just to spend time with me, and she even asked to work together on a group project. In class I always arrived early to brush up on notes, so she always came in and sat next to me, eventually coming to class early taking the seat right next to me (I eventually studied elsewhere and darted into class right before it started). The semester continued on, Annie always looking for more opportunities to see me.

When the semester ended, I was back at the "House from Hell" after being exiled from the dorms for the holiday. I happily studied away my days in the upper room. On this evening shortly after Christmas, I took a break from my studies to rearrange my room a bit. Whilst moving a heavy steel cabinet, my cell phone rang. It was Annie.

"Do you want to go to a movie?"

The call was odd. We never did anything directly social. Sure, we (with others in a group) had some dinners with the local chapter of our chemistry club, but never did we do anything merely social; it wasn't a scene I took any interest in. I didn't want to go, but had a spine like a jellyfish in those days. I needed an excuse to say no, and I looked for them. I had only an ace up my sleeve: that I was stranded in Saegertown without a car.

"I'll pick you up," she said.

Driving from Erie to Saegertown for a movie and then repeating the trip to go home was more than I would ever do for anyone. She insisted, so I reluctantly agreed to go see a movie. While there was a movie theater in Meadville, she wanted to go back up to Erie, so we saw a film and then headed back to Saegertown.

"Is there somewhere we can park for awhile?" she asked.

I wasn't too naive to know what she might want to do. I did...but didn't want to "park" for a while. But here in Saegertown where the population is slightly larger than an Amish village, but spread over far more farmhouses, I could think of a dozen places to park. We first tried the parking lot where I contemplated casting myself to the bottom a couple years prior, but there was too much snow. While anywhere off the main road would likely do, I directed her instead to where we had a few acres in the middle of the woods. The road to access our little "neighborhood" was already in the middle of nowhere, and one had to know exactly where to turn to find our access road that resembled a pull off. We headed down to the actual pull off just before having to cross the stream in the car. She left the van running for the heat and looked at me and smiled. I was about as much for conversation as I usually was, so after a few minutes of small talk, she planned her next move.

"Do you want to get into the back seat?"

Annie drove a van, and that meant a very spacious backseat. My milquetoast behavior sent me into the backseat with her, though I didn't really want to do much. I wasn't attracted to Annie in the slightest. While I can't say she was ugly, she didn't meet the requirements I would be looking for in a date. On top of that, she was double my age.

I had a deep-seated morality that came from somewhere unknown to me. While I was certainly not a paragon of purity, especially concerning sexual matters, I wanted to preserve "normal" sexual experiences for a time I would be committed and married. But a conflict arose in my mind. What if that never happened? What if I never got the chance? A part of my mind wanted to explore female anatomy further than I had with Shannon a few years earlier. Perhaps I could be persuaded into a game of "middle school baseball," and I was happy to strike out while heading home. That could maintain just enough purity to keep my conscience at bay.

I didn't have a lot of time to weigh all these arguments. Pretty much as soon as we made it to the back seat, Annie attacked my face. It was worse than a horny dog grabbing the leg of a confused child. Since it was a number of years since I had kissed a girl, I was captured by the moment and all the considerations melted away. It was like alcohol subduing the inhibitions. I wanted as much as I could get, and she wasn't shy! The only saving grace to my feeble attempt at purity was the ways of a woman, of which she was experiencing her monthly time. We did everything else that could have been done in that van. It was lovely... and horrible. I wanted it again, but never again.

That night at home I experienced relaxation and conflict all at the same time. I failed in my personal plans, but loved the art of failure. I hated myself, but was content[1]. It wasn't the same conflict in my mind that I experienced when I was used for other people's pleasure, after all, this was fully consensual, but I became mad at myself for my own failure to keep self control.

After a few days keeping myself busy with reading and studying, I took a break to be on the computer. The speakers beeped a request through ICQ. Was it my cousin pinging something funny, or my friend in the math department saying hi? Of course it was Annie. She pinged a message to see if I was online, and I said I was. She started typing small talk before inviting me to a "chat room session" which was a more rapid and live way to pass messages. In this rapid-paced room, her messages became overtly sexual. She was typing her own romance novel receiving feedback and instructions as I followed her lead. We penned a two-authored smut book in a short ten minutes time that might have put *50 Shades of Grey* to shame. It was a "write your own adventure" of the most base type. NSYNC had not yet released *Digital Getdown*, but I engaged in my one and only experience with what is now called "Cyber Sex."

A few days later I received an email from Annie asking if wanted to go to her house for New Years. Her invitation brought the conflict back to my mind. From the night parking

---

1 Romans 7:15

and the "Digital Getdown" I knew her intentions. Not under the influence of intoxicating kisses, I composed myself to think. I went for a long walk to think about the issues.

Many messages ran through my mind. At first, my desire to not spend New Years at the "House from Hell" beckoned any invitation, and I didn't have anyone calling up inviting me over. The desire to have one more night of peace away from that horrible place, counting the days when the dorms would once again be open. If I didn't have an inkling that Annie would jump my bones, the decision would be easy, but by now the time of the woman would have passed. As I weighed the decisions, I also prided myself on my mental discipline. I was convinced that I went further than I wanted on the first night because I wasn't prepared for what she wanted to do. Being more prepared now, I would be able to resist temptations. I made up my mind: I would go to Annie's house, but I wouldn't engage in any sexual activity. I felt strong as I walked down the street at night. I felt my strength and perseverance.

She picked me up in the late afternoon on New Year's Eve and we drove back to her house. We cooked a pizza and ate that while watching a movie. I kept my distance, perching myself on the chair and flipping through *Feynman's Lectures on Physics* like I was at my brother's house avoiding the wacky tobaccy. By the end of the movie I was on the couch because she asked me to move over there, and by the end of the film she was practically on top of me. Once the credits rolled, she attacked my face again. Kissing didn't cross the lines of my predecision, so I participated freely, becoming drunk on the sensations. My perfectly clear decisions on the dark and lonely road became muddled by hormonal influence. What yelled "only so far, then stop" faded into "wow I like this." She stopped kissing.

"Let's go upstairs," she said.

I followed her up the steps like a lamb to the slaughter of my conscience. She spared no time and was naked before I fully entered the room. I did the only thing that came natural to a twenty-year-old under the influence of hormones. A naked temptress can overwhelm the best laid plans of a sound mind, and my conscience became a slaughter right there on the alter of her bed[1]. We could never return to being mere study partners again.

During the following semester, I carried a burden I couldn't explain. Annie decided that I belonged to her and she would try to bring me food and even clothes. She pestered me on the phone in my dorm room to stop up "for just a minute." I relented. She came up with a bag full of clothes! She said my clothes were "not in style," as if a sound wardrobe were high on my list of priorities.

Having gone to bed one night, it was thus easier to keep doing it, though after a few times, I found a girlfriend as an excuse to keep away from Annie. On one interesting conversation we had, she even told me she was a Christian, and she even invited me to church. So here was a "Christian" woman who seduced a celibate atheist into sex. I had experienced another reason to see Christians as hypocrites, and why I was better off by myself. I didn't need a God!

---

1 Proverbs 7:22-27

A Dreamers Man in a Dreamers Land

March 4, 2000

An outcast man in an outcast land, suspicious from the skin
And then more unknown from deep within
What was it about him, he tried hard never to touch anyone
But in the end, the few would see
The few would see the unknown attraction that held them tight to him
Whatever he may do
The few could get in past his only weakness, Why? He didn't know
Where? He wished he knew
Whatever he did, they always came back, like pests upon a crap
They feed off the feelings
Why were these people so attracted? What did he do?
Why did he attract? He shouldn't.

Smarter Than the Average Christian

Living on campus was great in many respects, but I often needed to escape. While I took my job as a live-in tutor seriously and was generally approachable (by introverted standards), there were times I had to get away. Mike and I remained good friends after Remy took off to travel the world with his Christian group. Since Mike lived across the street from campus, about once a week we hung out by the lake. We mostly talked life and philosophy. This arrangement, which usually happened on the eve of organic chemistry exams, irritated my peers as they took over the student study lounge for a several hour chemistry binge. All while I took off for several hours to hang with my friend...and I still pulled the higher grade.

While I didn't actively study as much as my classmates, I learned over the last few years how to study with maximum efficiency. Usually my studying came in the form of hypnosis and meditation. I learned these skills back in high school and honed them to study by the middle of my college career. This approach allowed my semi-conscious mind to work out the problems and figure out the gaps in my learning. The arrangement left me rested, meaning I required fewer hours of sleep, but able to recall the concepts, particularly since I often placed myself in a similar trance during the exam to maintain focus.

Now in my third year in college, my dedication to the god of education produced fruit yielding protection and opportunity; things I only dreamed of a few years prior. If experience were the supreme indicator, nothing could rattle my dedication to academia. Through my studies, I received a job, a free dorm room, and a position that placed me over many of my fellow class mates. And I lived in that pride and in my successes. I didn't need to spend hours on end studying organic chemistry. I chose instead to go hang out with Mike.

On these nights, I passed by the glass doors to the study room where my peers wrestled with S_N2 reactions and organic nomenclature. I was on the way down to Mike, who waited in the circle outside for me. We stopped at the local convenience store to fill up large cups full of fake, sugary cappuccino and drove over to the lake. He parked his old, maroon Dodge Caravan a few blocks from the little cottage we used to rent and we stared over the waters. This regular pattern fueled many debates.

From our spot, we talked about a lot of things. We discussed the merits of education on the decisions of people. We talked about music and the impact it holds over our lives, and we talked about the old days in Edinboro and Saegertown, Remy and Jake, and anything else we might want to talk about. But one subject we rarely discussed was God. We used to talk about religion, but Mike got sick of always losing the debate.

Mike's parents raised him as a Christian kid, and even now in his later high school years, he kept a firm, but ill-informed, grasp on faith. We talked about God many times and in many ways in the past, but he could never answer my arguments: "If there is a good God, why do people suffer?"

My argument predicated itself on the statements that God is all loving and all powerful. Love is not abuse, being forced to live with violent people and those who incessantly teased you. Love is not a raw deal in life. If God is truly all powerful and all loving, clearly he would want the best for everyone. Mike had experienced a life I only dreamed was possible: two parents, a stable family, general personal safety, and a training ground for future responsibilities. He never had an argument other than saying that, "God's ways are mysterious." But what was mysterious to him was illogical to me.

I asked another question, "If God created everything, why is there evidence for evolution?" I was keen to point out the fossil record and what the atheist scientists of the day said. Since education was my god, I saw all the evidence that pointed to a transitional species that archaeologists just haven't found yet. Mike was no match for an arrogant college science major and he never even tried to refute me, but he held onto his faith, which to me, looked like he threw his brains in the garbage can.

My other favorite argument against God was the same statement I used on the kids in my neighborhood, "If there is a God, strike me down dead, now!" I yelled. God never did...so He didn't exist. Mike just said that it might not be in my best interest to strike me dead. Of course I went right back up to my previous argument: If God had my best interest in mind... Again, Mike was silenced. After a while, we established an agreement not to talk about God: I didn't want to hear it, and he couldn't defend his faith.

We didn't need to talk about God to have a good friendship. My new position on campus coupled with my freedoms from home were all served by my learning, and for me, education was the ticket to a good life. Mike couldn't argue with my point. He had experienced first hand the cruelness that William exhibited, and he had a general sense that his wayward brother cast off education while his other brother, who was a nice kid, took his schooling seriously. He saw how much better my life was after dedicating myself to my learning. I explained in detail how I used my knowledge of meditation and hypnosis to study, how that cemented the knowledge into my mind, and how I was able to pull out the highest grades in the class while the rest of them were behind in the dorms studying. Thus, to my argument that education is the means to a successful life, engaging in my new age practices increased that, and thus, I didn't need a God.

The Filthy Drink

I was never into the stupidity of drugs or drunkenness, but I did consume small amounts of alcohol from time to time. My experiences putting down the filthy drink showed me a potential for addiction, so I made a personal decision by the end of college not to drink alcohol nearly at all. My father, after all, was an alcoholic and the few times we did meet, it was only ever at bars. I only saw him sober three times in my life, and the drink didn't eradicate his problems.

I was never enticed by the party life because college was a time to learn, not live it up. The few times I would drink occurred when I stayed at my brother's house after our shifts at the restaurant. Those evenings, I would nurse a wine cooler for an hour or more. I liked the flavor, and the alcohol content is very low in those drinks. At this point, the illegality of drinking a cooler under age was clearly masked by the far more illegal things going on by the young men there to get high. Since I controlled myself never to drink too many wine coolers, I felt justified in my decision.

My dedication to remain sober-minded was upheld on my twenty-first birthday. My brother took me out to a restaurant where I had my first legal drink. It was more concentrated than I was interested in, and while I took a few sips over the course of a full meal, I left most of it behind. My brother knew I wasn't into getting drunk. We left there and went to a bar where his band had often played. We each had a wine cooler over the course of an hour of catching up on life. As it turns out, his friend was bar tending that afternoon and upon learning it was my twenty-first birthday, she brought me over a shot of Jack Daniel's whiskey. I smelled the volatility of the alcohol and determined that a shot of whiskey was not in my interest, so as we prepared to go, she came over to the table seeing the shot untouched. She looked at my brother and commanded, "Make him drink that!"

He chuckled. His friend didn't realize that would be an impossible task. While my brother tried time over time to get me to use drugs or drink unto drunkenness, he had recently given up on that. After his times trying to stone me in high school, he gave up after another of his pot-head parties; a situation he was still smarting from. It occurred after work one day when he had all his friends over like usual. We all sat in a big circle playing *Soul Blade* on the Playstation. The controllers traversed one direction around the circle while a bowl pipe traveled in the opposite direction. Like a sore thumb, I sat in the middle of this party reading a biochemistry textbook. The bowl came to him and he breathed in his puff, holding it in until the laughing cough expelled the smoke. He passed the bowl to me. I looked down on the pipe and up to his face, then our eyes both trained on the pipe again and then back to our eyes. I closed my biochemistry book and passed it to him...he has never offered me drugs again!

"If you can make him drink that," he replied, "I'll give you a million dollars."

He might have been morbidly curious to see what her doomed-to-fail approach might be. She didn't realize she was trying to reason with a prideful, arrogant, unreasonable person, but still she tried.

"When I turned twenty-one," she said, "my parents lined up twenty-one shots and I wasn't allowed to leave the bar until I drank them all."

The Filthy Drink

Disbelief of this new level of irrational insanity flooded my mind. I actually had to formulate a response and the clock stopped as three people all darted glances between ourselves. I finally found my words.

"If you actually thought you had to obey such a foolish command, I'm glad I'm not as stupid as you are."

After dropping my bomb, I left the bar.

Now being legal, more opportunities to drink presented themselves. On one instance, I was going to spend the evening at a friends house. Rex called me up before leaving Edinboro to ask if I can get a bottle of Vodka. I said I would be happy to if he could run to the store for some orange juice. I decided to swing by the house to grab the bottle of peach schnapps that had been in the cupboard for over a decade.

Upon grabbing the bottle, mother became unusually irrational about alcohol. She insisted that I don't take liquor with me to Rex's house, a surprisingly noble concern from a women who never said anything about her husband pulling guns on me. But I was over twenty-one, and I made up my mind. Not only did I make up my mind about taking alcohol to my friends house, but I also made up my mind about how much I would drink. I never wanted to be drunk.

Rex found booze himself in college and loved getting hammered even before he could legally drink. I came in the door, handing him the Vodka. He poured a shot glass and downed it in a second. He poured a second and passed it my way.

"I don't drink to get drunk," I said.

"Suit yourself," he replied and downed the second one, too. He wouldn't take convincing that I couldn't be pushed beyond my limits. He happily mixed his screwdrivers and became quite drunk, but I happily mixed a tablespoon of so of my schnapps into a cup of orange juice for just enough flavor to enjoy the game of cards we played throughout the evening.

While these rare events were generally harmless, I started noticing alcohol and other potentially addictive mediums can capture us in subtle ways. When I kept a sober mind, I spotted the "dependency creep" that beckons many people into various deadly traps. The first observation possibly leading into dependency occurred during my senior year in college when I was battling a case of "Senioritus".

After seven difficult semesters and the full prospect of passing this final one also with exceptional grades, I took to relaxing on Monday nights. This semester I managed to only have one Tuesday class, and occasionally the professor canceled it because we were routinely ahead of schedule. These wonderful evenings I gathered the week's worth of dirty clothes, rented a bunch of movies, and bought a four pack of Jack Daniels Coolers. I headed to the "house from hell" and barricaded myself in my room, with my glorious entertainment system, and organized class notes, studied, all while watching movies and drinking down the coolers. In this arrangement, I still kept my personal commitment to never be drunk, but I started to see myself "needing" the coolers on a Monday night. The whole idea of needing anything didn't sit well with me, particularly since alcohol was involved. I pondered this thought in my mind.

A second incident in the same year gave me the final perspective. On this evening after work, I decided upon invitation, to go to a bar with my brother and his friend. Both men knew my desires and my personal limits. Since my brother wasn't a drinker, there was little peer pressure possible in this arrangement. I had my usual wine cooler, but as we tarried longer at the bar than I thought we might, I ordered something else a little stronger. I still drank it slowly, but I wasn't used to the strength of a hardened drink. I didn't get drunk on the rum and coke, but it was able to buzz me a bit. At that moment, I realized I had lost a firm grip on my rational mind, and was at risk of losing myself further into alcohol.

My final perspectives on these weighty thoughts are that the risks involved in drinking far outweigh any rewards. I personally needed to keep my mind about me, and following the path I was on would surely compromise my convictions. I had to stay sober minded to take care of myself, no one else was there for me, not even God.

Brush With Mortality

Death is a part of life, but it is that part of life we like to shove under the rug and forget about. One night after family Christmas when I was in the first grade, tucked warmly in my lower bunk of my bed, wrapped in my new blanket and admiring a top that lit up when spun, I pondered death. The dark, frightening thought overshadowed my joy like an ice cube materializing in my little safe place. I was going to die. What would become of my little top or my blanket? What would happen after that? I drifted off to sleep in terror, the same terror felt by every little kid at some point in their life. But like a mist, it faded away and I never really thought about death again until my grandma's failing health made her departure imminent. That happened in high school. After she finally died, however, the darker forces in the world seemed to open the floodgates to keep the possibility of death as a bitter taste on the tip of my tongue. It became clear to me that no one, old or young, is promised tomorrow.

Being a loner with a sensible mind, I rarely participated in the stupid popular recklessness among my peers, but at the hands of my brother and his cohort, my life was placed in danger many times, particularly involving automobiles. In those days, the law permitted a minor to drive his friends around, and my generation was probably the reason such things were restricted. The first driver among his peer group liked to drive full speed through stop signs only to slam on the brakes half way through. His regular joke response always accompanied laughter as if his stupid antics were somehow comical. That ended the day his laughter was subdued by a vulgar "S---!" as I felt the car jolt in an unusual way. On this day, a car actually drove through the right of way causing our land yacht to enter a high-speed collision course. Our foolish driver slammed on the brakes, maneuvering the car between the oncoming van and the previously ignored stop sign. We narrowly avoided a crash and he became the best driver in the world for the rest of the way to school.

My brother had another friend that was supposed to drive me to Roberts house one summer day, and also started messing around behind the wheel. He liked to start swerving his car back and forth between the lanes. My protests only egged him on to increase the speed. I finally sat quietly until they stopped at the Giant Eagle that was roughly behind our house. I jumped out of the car and started walking home. They tried to get me back into the car so they wouldn't get in trouble from Mom.

"You drive like a lunatic!" I protested.

"I only mess around on back roads," he answered.

This sentiment was little comfort to me since Robert lived in the middle of the country. Having no desire to be found dead in a ditch on the back roads of McKean, Pennsylvania, I walked the rest of the way back home.

My brother attempted to kill us another day shortly after receiving his license. On the way to school after a detour into the boondocks to pick up his friend, they got nice and high for the drive to school. He turned into Crane road, a long, straight road leading back onto the main drag to school. He opened up the engine, hastening down the road at speeds nearing that of a small aircraft. Ahead down the road, an old Thunderbird pulled through the intersection and stalled out. After a few seconds seeing the car wasn't moving, slowed by the power of his magical herbs, he finally slammed on the brakes, squealing out the tires, and losing control over the vehicle. We skidded off the road, missing the Thunderbird, and bouncing instead through a freshly harvested corn field. The car slammed to a stop, all three of us whirring in a dizzy haze. We survived, and the car didn't sustain any damage either. I started taking the bus again after that day.

Near misses aside, in the following years, six of my friends and acquaintances met death. In the summer after I graduated high school, the phone rang. I left my room to see Mom frantically making some phone calls. A loud, "NO!!!!" pierced the tiny cottage on the lake, jolting me into getting involved. Mom's best friend, Pat, who gave us a place to stay when we moved back to the east, had just passed away.

Pat's death was sudden. While never the paragon of health, she was Mom's age, and like an aunt to me. We grew up with her kids, making it over to her house every few months. We swam in her pool, had picnics and parties at her huge house, and generally enjoyed the times with her kids. Now she was dead. We made it to the funeral, hugged the kids, and cried over a young person's death. Words couldn't express what I felt. Within only six months, her eighteen-year old son also died. We grew up together and he was the first person my own age I knew who died.

Robert joined them on the other side about a year later. After dropping out of school, I only talked to him on the phone a few times. The last time we talked, he had two broken legs. He was sick of the low-level high afforded by pot and branched out to some more potent drugs. One day he took some acid and saw visions of the Grim Reaper coming for him. In his attempt to get away, he jumped out the second story window in his bedroom, shattering both legs at the bottom. In the hospital, he loved pushing the button for more morphine, so the doctors removed his ability to self-medicate. Once healed up, he sought out heroine for the ultimate high. One spring night, coming off his buzz, with the pain of his failing life refocusing before his eyes, he couldn't bear the sight. He placed a single bullet through his head. When I heard of his death through Jake, I sat down to think about all our adventures in middle and high school. He gave me some of my best times, but he also provided a metaphor for how we often move on to other friends as our interests train in different directions. I couldn't dwell on death, and keep myself alive, so I played a Metallica tape in his honor, and moved on with my life.

Robert wasn't the only friend I lost due to complications with heroine. I worked with Gary at the restaurant while I was a cook and baker. He was a good worker, always diligent in his tasks, and never wasting any time. In my recollections, Gary loved life, had a good relationship with his sister and parents, and always demonstrated a good attitude. In the fall, he went off to college and met up with a new group of friends who accepted him, even though they were into things he found a little distasteful at first. Like Alipius in Rome, his friends dragged him off to taste the terrible wonders in life. They showed him the highs of heroine. Gary took the drug and immediately loved it, taking it a few more times with his new college friends. He didn't know he shared a needle with an HIV positive person. He developed an unknown illness and the doctor tested him for HIV. Gary tested positive. The virus grabbed him quickly and started in with early complications. He feared a life of the unknown, fearing what his friends and family might think, and chose instead to end his life in the same manner as Robert a few years earlier.

Death apparently had an open season on our restaurant staff because another co-worker also died only a few months after Gary. He worked in the pantry, a department separated by the bakery only with a short divider. The nature of the close working quarters made the bakers and pantry workers all friends, so I talked to him any time he worked. He partied a great deal, like my brother, but came into his job taking it seriously. His death was as sudden as Gary's. I worked with him one Sunday afternoon then headed back to the college for my week of courses, returning Friday night finding that he had died. His death didn't relate to parties, but was a sudden infection of some kind. His passing reminded me that even people who don't make stupid life decisions also find death without provocation.

Around the same time these two friends passed, we lost a fellow worker at the Planetarium. Not only did I work with Erin, but we also graduated high school together. He was a nice boy who moved into the district in the latter part of high school. Erin was quiet and mostly stayed out of everyone's way; he was a clean-cut kid that you just wanted to see succeeding in life. Like me, he joined the planetarium staff. We made a good team, him often leading the elementary school programs through the night sky while I toured them through the biology museum and the other attractions offered by Cooper Hall.

I found out about Erin's death when I went to Edinboro for some errands on a Saturday. I bumped into a mutual friend and was told about his passing. I made my way over to the planetarium to talk to Dr. Daniels. I arrived just in time to go the funeral home with him. We paid our respects and then talked to his mom to get the details.

It was a simple car accident, something that could take any of us off this earth at any time. In his case, he passed a car and over-corrected, throwing his car into a ditch at a rapid enough speed to spin out of the control. EMS pronounced him dead at the scene. Once again, no drugs, no bad decisions, just twisted fate, cruel to the victim, cruel to their friends. How could a good God let something like this happen?

All these deaths in a short period of time, some the fruit of wicked ways, others cruel fate, all showed me that our time on earth is limited. What happens then? I had a religious system that made me more powerful here on earth, but not one that had anything to say about an afterlife. I wrestled with the questions about annihilation, reincarnation, heaven, and hell. I didn't believe in the latter, and the former made me wonder. Rather than think about these things, I busied myself with my own survival, deciding not to think about the consequences that would happen if I failed.

Found by Jesus

I permitted Myself to be sought
by those who did not ask for Me;
I permitted Myself to be found
by those who did not seek Me.
I said, 'Here am I, here am I,'
To a nation which did not call on My name.
Isaiah 65:1

The Time Has Come

My plan to escape the family was operating efficiently. On that cold February night during my freshman year, in lieu of suicide, I planned to pass through college with flying colors, leave, and never look back. Now in my senior year, I had been recognized as a successful and serious student, paid to teach others how to learn, and had just been given a full ride to graduate school. I had actually exceeded my expectations to this point, and I started making my preparations to disappear. For seven semesters I looked forward to becoming a ghost, then God Himself showed up and stood in my path.

He let me labor in my heart to keep me going. He was the fear who allowed me to find new energy I didn't know existed; energy I needed to stay alive so I could move on with the next part of my life. When He appeared, He transformed me into a whole new creature, a creature who knew that forsaking a family, even an abusive one, was only a last resort. Instead, God would teach me how to cope.

My new Master hunted me down. He was like a cat, however, toying with his prey. He let me go in a few steps that seemed right to me, and then He pulled me back. I belabored for years that I had outsmarted Him, but His meekness suddenly became brute force before my very eyes. He snatched my soul from the Devil, and only in retrospect did I see his plan for me.

The seed set firm in my soiled mind germinated somewhere between the summer and the start of my last semester in college. In the middle of the summer, Rex had planned to come over for the evening, but a guy he worked with asked him to a meeting to "have his own business" which was really a pitch for a popular multi-level marketing program. He was, of course, allowed to bring his friend. He called me up to tell me about this thing, expecting that I would not be interested so he could use my answer as an excuse not to go. In reality, I wasn't interested, but I didn't mind tagging along with Rex, so I said that I would go with him. He downplayed it again, talking about the need to wear a suit.

"I have a suit," I said. I didn't mention it was this horrible brown thing I had acquired for the occasion of Pat's funeral.

"OK," he answered.

Rex arrived looking sharp. His day job as a bank teller assured his suit fit perfectly and matched the current style. Mine, on the other hand, was out of place. Not only did the color resemble that of vomit, but it wasn't even tailored to my body size. To make it look all the more ridiculous, I put on my old tennis shoes with holes in both toes, proudly displaying my faded socks. It was our glorious "screw you" to corporate America.

The meeting itself was populated with lunatics. Everyone adorned fake smiles, detectable only to a person who had lived through as much misery as I had. They all talked about what a "great opportunity" this was and how we should "join today" so we had a future. I wasn't interested in the fakers, so I openly rejected their opportunity. Rex, on the other hand, decided to give it a try.

In December, he convinced me to join up, if for no other reason, than to get discounts on good vitamins. On the weekend before classes started, I ended up at one of their weekend seminars where I still thought everyone had lost their mind. They all kept talking about the importance of the optional Sunday morning meeting, but I wasn't interested. I was perceptive enough to see these people were Jesus Freaks, and I didn't want anything to do with religion. Rex, who used to be my partner in sin, now seemed to be more like these people, and he suggested I might go.

On the Sunday morning of the special, "optional" meeting, I stood in front of the mirror sliding up my horrible red tie, admiring my hideous appearance in the gaudy suit. I looked at Rex through the reflection of the mirror.

"I'll go to this thing," I said, "but don't expect anything."

"I won't," he said, smiling, as if he knew some secret I didn't know.

We filed in to the conference room in the Hyatt Regency at the Baltimore inner harbor. The room filled up quickly with smiling people who kept on greeting me, as I, in return, greeted their shoes with grunts. We took a seat, Rex putting me somewhere in the middle of the row, a conspiracy with his friends to keep me from fleeing early in the meeting. I knew this was a talk about God, and I wasn't interested. I was educated, about to go off for my doctoral degree. I was taught my academic plan would immediately make me successful, and I didn't need anything from these Jesus Freaks.

True to myself, I didn't hear a single word of the talk. I couldn't tell you today if it was "Hell and Brimstone" or "Everyone is Always Loved" monologue. Instead of listening, I spent my time counting the lights and ceiling tiles. Boredom led me to count everything twice, but the guy still kept on talking. *How long can he go on?*, I mused. I took up studying the patterns on the carpet. I learned every nuance, but the guy kept droning on. I started making observations...strange observations; not of the stage, but of the people sitting in the chairs.

I saw men with their arms around their wives. I never saw men treat their wives in such a manner. If that wasn't enough, they cuddled small children on their laps and didn't yell when their brood interrupted. The fake smiles of the first meeting were replaced by genuine gladness. People were actually happy in a way I had experienced only a few times before.

I first saw this type of genuine happiness in Mike and Remy. Even when things were not going as they wanted, they took a positive outlook on life, a contrast to my way of thinking. Mr. Hersh also showed this type of happiness. I saw it in his classroom and the times we talked outside of school. Dr. Daniels shared this expression, too. It was as if I saw each of these friends in the expressions of the strangers in the chairs.

This look was foreign to me. It was the feeling I longed to have, so I ran through a checklist in my mind to see where it came from. First, I topped most of these people in education. Only a few college-and-beyond educated people sat in the meeting. Most of the people I had met in this group had only attended high school and a little bit of college; nothing as impressive as my biochemistry curriculum.

I considered their opportunities next. Maybe they had better jobs–but they were all at this business meeting to learn how to get rid of their jobs! Also, my dad had a lot of money and that never solved his problems. I kept drifting back in my mind to one point I had repeatedly suppressed: they had God. The one thing all these people had, along with all the nicest people I had met in my past, was that they all talked about God, or rather, Jesus.

That couldn't be! I yelled to myself.

Right at that moment there was a commotion. Everyone in the room stood up. I joined them so that I didn't stand out. I longed to blend into this crowd, to have this feeling of happiness, but I certainly wanted to leave God out of the mix.

The guy on the stage said that anyone who wanted to accept Jesus should come forward. Several people started walking toward the front, but I didn't. I didn't want to "accept Jesus," whatever that meant. I stood in total defiance. I didn't follow along with the prayer he said, but rather, I stood there cursing God and Jesus in my mind, declaring myself too smart for religion. It was Custer's last stand, Hiroshima versus Little Boy...but Jesus was the bomb.

I hadn't heard a single word of the guy on stage, and frankly, it wouldn't have mattered if I had. The seed that germinated in my mind was planted long ago by the friendships of Remy and Mike, Mr. Hersh and Dr. Daniels. It was their prayers that caused the leaflets to peek through the soil of my mind on that illuminating day. It wasn't the result of any prayer from the front to "give myself to Jesus". I am not sure to this day if I said a "prayer of salvation" but something clicked in that moment and I knew that God was real, that Jesus was God, and that He died to save me from my sins. I didn't choose Him, He chose me. He rode his white horse of the apocalypse into my black, sin-soiled heart, kicked out the demons, and set up camp. Everything *had* to change from that day forward.

Through this bombshell revelation He instantly crumbled every presupposition I had about God. I finally made my proclamation:

"I was wrong!" I said.

Those were the hardest words for an arrogant fool to say.

"I was wrong," I repeated again. I collapsed into the chair and started a crying binge lasting over twelve hours. In that moment, I saw I wasn't a victim of the consequences in my life, but an active participant in what God had called *sin*. I knew the challenges I faced were mine to deal with, but now I had a God to guide me through life. In that moment, He showed me a new direction. He showed me that the manner I lived was wrong, not from a societal perspective, but from a truth perspective. He is truth, everything else is a lie.

White Washed heart
July 30, 2004

I lived a life of sinful toil
All actions spent in vain
My iniquity spun out of control
Destroying my heart for You.

I read the words of Your Word
But I could not comprehend
I could recall the stories
But my heart was dead.

A hurtful sin was carved
Deep into my very soul
Destroying my innocence
And separating me from You.

As I ran, I ran in sin
Seeking to escape Your call
But wherever I ran, You were there
Oh, Lord, where can I escape You?

Though destroyed to my very soul
I sought in shame to flee
With my damaged heart broken
I only wanted to run.

I felt separated, alone, and scared
I sought only to get away
But wherever I ran, You were there
Prompting me to stop.

At last I quit running
I let the battle rage on my heart

Found by Jesus

I stood up, rejected, then accepted
I fell down and began to cry.

Your work in me began, Oh, Lord
But it did not come all at once
I sought to escape my sin
But I forgot to do it in You.

But you kept me close, conditioning me
Incubating me for Your work
I thought I could not escape
The wretched sins of my past

But You did more then just forgive
You grabbed them up at last
You reached to where I could not reach
And You removed that terrible thorn.

For I began to grow though the thorn remained
And I sought hard for it to be gone
I wished, I hoped, but I forgot to pray
I am fallen, after all.

When I was still lost
You knew best what I needed
I wanted that painful thorn gone
That pain with roots so deep.

Oh, Lord, You are the master of all!
You reached inside of me
You reached down to where I could not reach
And You pulled the root out of me!

You white washed my heart, Oh, Lord!
You did it all by Your hand
For as hard as I tried, I failed
But You cleansed my thorn from me.

The Time Has Come

You did the impossible work
You raised me from my grave
You pulled me up and gave me a heart
And You put a dream in me

And, Lord, I am forever in debt
For Your saving grace
And I vow to You my dream
Shall come to completion!

Grow the seeds I plant for You
Reap a kingdom of Grace
From the dream You put in me
Lord, I praise You forever!

Be Ye Sanctified

A Christian who doesn't grow into the likeness of Christ is likely not a Christian at all. Let's unpack that statement and clarify it before I risk being branded a heretic so early into my testimony. First, I am under no illusion that we reach perfect, sinless life this side of heaven. Secondly, we do not instantly become perfect Christian saints once the Holy Spirit takes up residence inside us. The lag between our salvation and when we really start looking like Christians is a stage of growth I liked to call the "incubation period". Much like a child takes time to grow up, Christians must be given a measure of grace as God works in their life. Maturing in Christ, however, will begin from the first day of a person's conversion.

On the first day of our new-found faith, we are a new creature[1]. That means God works a miracle in our lives; a single small down payment with the promise of final glorification[2] when we have reached eternity with Christ.

In my case, I had an instant change in my countenance toward other people. Leading up to my salvation, the callousness in my heart caused me to readily push everyone away. I am surprised that anyone actually wanted to spend time with me. The most shining example of my attitude toward people was the time I made the line server at the restaurant cry over blueberry muffins.

---

1 2 Corinthians 5:17
2 Philippians 1:6

We served the cherished muffins on Saturday and Sunday mornings. The closing baker made the muffins right at the end of the shift so they would be fresh and ready for the early customers. On this Friday night, we had plenty of strawberry muffins, which we served at dinner, and I had just pulled out a fresh batch of blueberry. I put them high up on the cooling rack and even covered them so they would be hard to see and hard to reach. But this line server did it anyway. When my back was turned, she ignored the proper muffins and took a tray of my new ones out...the ones for the morning shift. When I saw that she took those forbidden pastries out to the bar, I screamed at her until she cowered. The vulgarity spewing forth from my lips was enough to make a sailor blush. She retreated into the freezer to cry, and then returned there every once in a while to shed more frozen tears. The manager asked why she was crying in the freezer.

"Good," I declared arrogantly, "she deserves it for taking my fresh muffins."

Fast forward a few weeks, God did perform a miracle that day. "Please" and "thank you" replaced vulgar words in my vocabulary. I mostly remained silent in my bakery, afraid to alienate people or spread the gossip I heard from around the break table. The few times I finally spoke I was softer and gentler. Everyone noticed it.

I didn't instantly become changed; it was more like I became aware of the offenses I committed against people and grew the desire to care for them instead of making them cry. The times I slipped into the old patterns, I started feeling guilty about what I did. On one occasion when I arrived at my shift to close the bakery, I found they let the morning shift person go early to save on labor costs. I arrived and the place was a disaster zone. I got mad and demanded why I had to come in to such a mess. My old ways came out and vulgar words came to my lips again, and so brutaly that our boss, the most mild-mannered person you may ever meet, flipped me some double birds, returned some choice words, and slammed the door to leave for the day. For the first time, I was upset at the conflict, but it wasn't for what the boss said to me, it was actually for what I had said to him. This radical change pricked my conscience all night, and when I went in to close the store the following day, I asked to talk to the boss privately.

"I'm sorry for yesterday," I sheepishly said, an apology that would never have come a few months earlier. "I just became a Christian not long ago, and I am still learning. And I want to ask you to forgive me for my attitude."

Who is saying these things?, I pondered to myself.

"It's OK," he said, "I am a Christian myself. And I wondered about you...I have seen so much nicer an attitude in you lately."

Our relationship took leaps and bounds forward from that day on.

As I continued my walk in Christ, Annie was the next casualty to my new way of life. While we got together a few more times since our first sexual encounter, and even a few times after I became a Christian, the sexual pleasure drew colder and more violent to my conscience. I never "loved" her, but we had the whole "friends with bennies" thing going on.

While I wasn't a Christian through most of this, she always professed to be a believer. Still, my conscience, informed by reading my Bible, showed me that without marriage, sex wasn't permitted. I noticed a pattern that most of the sexual encounters we had, I was a willing participant, but she usually instigated the sin. Our last night showed me the total contradiction in living between two worlds[1]. That night we engaged in sexual activity without any protection, for reasons I didn't ask until after the event.

"I'm on the pill," she said.

"You don't believe in birth control," I replied. It was a fact I knew from all the studying together.

"I don't, but I took it for two reasons," she started explaining, "First, I am going on a mission trip in a few weeks and I want to be 'normal' and second, I am never sure when you're going to be around."

These words echoed in my newly growing Christian mind. God showed me my part in active sin here, and He also showed me how we people are so double minded[2] and how that will lead to our own destruction[3]. Here was a professing Christian who took birth control to both attend a mission trip for God and to commit fornication. And I was party to the sin. After that night, I committed not to ever see her again; for there is no returning to Eden[4], and there is no turning back to merely being friends once sexual activity occurs in a relationship. She called a month later and I said I would call her back, but I never did. And to to this day, I have never spoken to her again.

At this point in my Christian walk, I had never heard the term *Sanctification*, but that's exactly what I experienced. Like a child into his adolescence, unsure of the ways of his body, I walked down paths I didn't understand to become more like Christ.

---

1 Revelation 3:16
2 James 4:8
3 Revelation 22:15
4 Genesis 3:24

For me, it started when I committed myself to read the Bible. I started seeing things I did which were contrary to the ways in the Bible[1]. During this time, I started observing the inputs I inserted into my mind[2]. I looked at the movies and music that existed in my collection, and I looked at the files on my computer. I starting removing the entertainment that didn't line up with the Bible. While I never collected anything like pornography, I did collect some stand up comedy routines and other vile television shows. I decided to delete those files from the computer, dispose of movies and music that didn't fit the bill, and I chose to distract myself with cleaner entertainment. It wasn't that everything I partook of was "Christian", but it was certainly not full of the evil vile I had once enjoyed[3].

After disposing of horrible entertainment, I started looking at the myriad of sentimental belongs that I had lugged from house to house in my quest to hold tight onto periods of my life that I also longed to forget. I can't quite explain it. Perhaps the things we hold onto are like the constant replaying in our minds of our abuses; the same ones we might imagine making better choices to avoid. But these things; objects, mostly meaningless, kept bringing up my past to me, and it wasn't a past full of sunshine and rainbows. I saw these objects as idols; things preventing me from seeing God because I had to filter everything through them first. I took them out, examined them carefully, and one by one, tossed them into the dumpster outside my apartment.

As if by coincidence, right when I started pondering my filthy life and cleaning it up, I was given a subtle reminder to the cleansing power of God through a sermon delivered by my

---

[1] Ephesians 4:17
[2] Romans 12:2
[3] I have written about Christians and media entertainment in my book *I AM not Amused*.

pastor. He examined the life of King Josiah from 2 Chronicles 34. This king sought God for four years before first starting to clean up his life. Here I was, the consummate overachiever, cleaning my life up after only three!

Once I did the things like he had: cleaned up the idols, removed the ability to consume bad materials, sought God in all ways possible, I likewise started experiencing amazing things in my walk with Jesus Christ. It was like lights were turned on in my mind and the power of God started flowing through me. This phase in my Christian walk took about three years to start. It was a growth spurt in my faith, a sign that God really was real.

To conclude this chapter, I hear the cries that many of my readers are screaming out in their own mind, "I'm stuck right here. Help me move into this maturity!"

The principles come from Romans 12:1-2:

> *Therefore I urge you, brethren, by the mercies of God, to present your bodies a living and holy sacrifice, acceptable to God, which is your spiritual service of worship. And do not be conformed to this world, but be transformed by the renewing of your mind, so that you may prove what the will of God is, that which is good and acceptable and perfect.*

First, we must be willing to give up ourselves to be sacrificed to His service. While we wont find ourselves bundled up like Isaac on Mount Moriah[1], we will find that many things we used to enjoy become off limits as we give our desires to God. The next phase is also represented in this verse: *renew your mind*.

We are transformed by God's power through a cooperation with the Holy Spirit in our lives. He teaches us what we need to

---

1 Genesis 22

know[1] through Bible study and prayer. To renew our minds, we must stop the tap of sinful things we feed our head, preferring instead to dwell on the things of God. This is accomplished by replacing sinful habits and entertainment with holy ones instead. We need to, in the words of Paul, focus on *whatever is true, whatever is honorable, whatever is right, whatever is pure, whatever is lovely, whatever is of good repute, if there is any excellence and if anything worthy of praise, dwell on these things (Philippians 4:8).*

The second step is to learn more about God. A single sermon per week is not enough to grow, particularly if you came from a wretched life such as mine. I started consuming sermons. You can also turn on Christian radio stations that play sermons and listen to who is there. Christian television is a little more suspect; more false teachers have television ministries than radio ministries, so use discernment and seek a mentor to help you sort out what is good and what is bad teaching. Listen to multiple sermons per day if possible.

Finally, dedicate yourself to the Christian disciplines. I place this last because it is the hardest to do, but it is also the most critical step. The two primary disciplines are prayer and Bible Study. These together will teach you the most about God. Bible study gives us the mind of God while prayer enlightens us to the heart of God. When we combine these principles together, we are able to grow into the likeness of Christ.

Sorry this is not a simple list to follow, but neither is the Christian life easy[2]. The reality is, growing into the likeness of Christ, the process of sanctification, is not easy, but it is commanded. Every person who is legitimately saved will become more like Christ, will separate from the world, and will dwell on God's Word like a thirsty deer longs for streams of

---

1 John 14:26
2 John 15:18-25

water[1]. Dedication to God is a discipline, not an easy list of simple steps.

Temptations

August 5, 2004

A decision is set firm
In the depths of my mind
I go through life aware
Of what to set behind
I talk and preach
Of what I do not do
And say what others
Should not pursue
I live my life with
My mind on straight
And set out from the beginning
With what to hate
A passion burns
Within my heart
Of what I never
Wish to start
And I move in life
With a place to point
To a place where
I shall not disappoint

And that one thing
Stares me in the face
And without the strength of Christ
I'll do what I distaste.

---

1 Psalm 42·1

No Love

June 11, 2003

Lips to kiss, and a tongue to feel
A passion heats up with a moment
The occurrence happens in so short a time
With no time for a thought of consent

As I move on, I think "this will be last"
If I don't move now, never again
Will I feel the sensation
Wanted by so many men

In past, you acted first
And I didn't want to go
But now caught up in my own reactions
It happened even though

Instigation rarely from me
Although I participated freely in act
The feelings and sensations there
But something from within has lacked

A drive in love is a must acquire
For time with you is just there
Nothing magic in the feeling
After done, I don't really care

Time again, opportune
I took the time to act my way
I realized while going on
That without love, this is not OK

I had an empty feeling
While preparing to release my stress

That feeling came when I realized
This is not for love, but Lust, I confess.

A Worker Approved

My process through sanctification culminated with a final call to service[1]. In His sovereignty, God even arranged a christening event – a final sendoff into the cruel world. At this time, about three years had passed since I had become a Christian. God had used that time to work on my heart. I learned about all the sinful things I had done in my past. I also learned about the personal consequences involved in coming from a dysfunctional home. God walked me through the steps I needed to do to leave behind the old patterns. I was a new creature[2], and He gave me new ways of making decisions.

My real struggle, I had learned, was that my abuses weren't my problem. The ways I had accosted God through my sin was my real struggle. Once I repented of my old ways and focused on God's word, I learned how to please Him through my actions[3]. He proved faithful to remove my sin upon my confession[4], and He set me free indeed once I learned the truth about our world[5].

At the conclusion of my period of self-discovery, I answered a call to work at the annual Vacation Bible School (VBS) program at church. I was already experienced with kids through babysitting in the old neighborhood, not to mention the four years I toured elementary school kids around our

---

1 Ephesians 2·10
2 2 Corinthians 5·17
3 Romans 12·1-2
4 1 John 1·9
5 John 8·32

building while working for the planetarium. We kicked off the week with a prayer dinner the night before the program began.

During the dinner, I met a couple at the church whom I talked with most of the evening. I shared my testimony, including many of the sordid details of my dysfunctional past. My new friends prayed over my old wounds, and God laid to rest the concerns of my past. I was healed of my dysfunction[1]. God sent me to a mission field, mostly with children—a callback to point kids to the real truth that I never had received: the opportunity to explore in my own childhood.

Our VBS program taught me many important lessons early in my ministry. As a guide, my task included leading the kids through the stations, keeping an eye on them, and meeting with each child to talk about the things they learned throughout the day.

I first learned about the importance of prayer. My lesson came to fruition about a month after the program concluded. One boy in the group came from a family much like I did. He didn't have any church experience or parents who knew anything about God. His neighbor, however, invited the kids to the program, and the parents didn't object. He reminded me so much of myself: reclusive, quiet, and angry at life.

My desire was for this boy to become a Christian, so I prayed through out the week for his salvation. God didn't agree with my prayers and for good reason. If that boy became a Christian during that week, I would certainly have thought that my ability or skill with the Gospel was the root cause. But men don't choose God on their own[2]; He first draws them[3]! After the event, I kept praying for this boy to be influenced by God. Any

---

1 James 5:15
2 Romans 3:10-18
3 John 6:44

answer at this point didn't have anything to do with me, but was all on God. About a month later, his mom became a Christian, so he now had a Christian influence in his life.

My work in VBS opened the door to other opportunities. For the first time in my life, my focus was removed from me and my problems; I started looking to help other people where I could, a complete opposite approach that had guided my life up to this point. I was offered a spot on a children's church team because of my work in VBS. I joined the team and worked with them for about a year. I eventually swapped working on that team for Sunday school. I preferred Sunday school better because I thought kids should be in the regular worship service, not pulled from families and isolated into their own little group to receive a different message from their parents.

My experiences in Sunday school gave me further lessons in ministry. The importance of having correct information while teaching is paramount. We will be judged harder for the lessons we teach[1], whether that be in an adult class or with little kids. This realization drove me to desire studying the fine details in the Bible, making deeper connections than I found in curricula cleverly designed for third graders.

No one ever told me that kids couldn't sit down to expositional Bible study using multiple supporting verses. And once I tried that approach, the kids learned more about the Bible in my Sunday school class than the older kids were learning in the youth group (according to the testimony of parents with children in both programs). My approach actually worked. The parents were thrilled, and my students knew more about the Bible than their peers from other churches. God appeared to be blessing my teaching style. My final lesson was that a Sunday school teacher should always be called by God, and

---
1 James 3:1

should be able to assemble their own notes using the Word and prayer as a means to create their lessons.

The more I worked for God, the more opportunities I found to serve Him[1]. Sometimes these opportunities came from people seeing that I served and they would give me a call on the phone to ask if I could fill their need. Other times, I felt it was God whom told me to start seeking out some of the opportunities. The later ones were always more blessed, but it opened up more lessons in my growing faith. This was the lesson on balancing spiritual disciplines.

I knew from my personal work before ministry that time in the Word studying the things I needed to know combined with prayer built me up. But working so much *for* God took away much of my time *with* God. I needed to relearn balance, so I took time several days a week during my lunch break as my time with Him. I read through the whole Bible and studied sections that I needed to personally spend time on. I found that re-balancing myself restored the personal growth and joy that started fading when I became too busy. Like clockwork, other opportunities presented themselves after I found this balance. I was able to help a local Chinese church teach their youth group, splitting the role with a youth pastor they had. I also joined the committee for the local Child Evangelism Fellowship chapter.

The two greatest blessings came when I followed God's lead. I offered two weeks a year to camp counseling in the summer, and I also became a community mentor. Camp is focused and powerful–for the kids and the counselors alike. I never met anyone at the camp who didn't finish the week more blessed for having taken the time, even on the challenging weeks.

---

1 Luke 12:48

The first week of camp impressed on me measures of grace. The first measure was shown to me. In the past, in the old neighborhood, I always told the kids that there wasn't a God. I denied Him, and those kids looked up to me for some reason. I shudder to think that my foolish, teenage words may have become a stumbling block to those kids[1]. Somehow, God saw me fit to lead a group of similarly aged children into a week of camp, trusting that I would give them the Gospel instead of taking it away.

The second measure of grace was toward other people. Working with kids is not always easy. They are little people, just like us, but they generally have less control over their emotions; they are more inclined to say what they are thinking, and that could mean a greater propensity to hurt us. I learned these lessons of grace through a dozen weeks of working with the kids. Sometimes they were the nicest and most behaved group of children one could imagine, while other times they seemed to descend directly from hell to test our patience. One week I had a kid whose background echoed something similar to David Pelzer. He lashed out in anger at nearly everyone, but with the support of the rest of camp, by the end of the week, the boy showed a calm demeanor. It took a lot of prayer, and the occasional social-worker hold to bring the boy into peace with the rest of camp. Whatever my situation, I praised God and learned more grace for other people; a lesson I was desperate to learn.

While camp was an intense ministry that lasted only a few weeks out of the year, I was also called to community mentoring. This service was rendered outside the church, something I consider necessary in the scope of the Great Commission[2]. My work in Big Brothers, Big Sisters spanned a

---

1 Matthew 18:6
2 Matthew 28:19-20

decade. I was matched with four kids in that span of time, but I reached dozens more through the program by inviting their friends into our time. Big Brothers, Big Sisters took me out of the sanitary church situations with good kids, usually two parent homes, and it placed me into a mission field of people without regard for the church. I mentored raw kids with real problems: kids who were a lot like me growing up. This presented an opportunity to show God's love to kids who were a lot like me.

All the kids I worked with had some degree of conflict at home. Some of the matches were rather short lived for one reason or another. The final match I had lasted for several years, until the kid wasn't a kid any more. He is still a friend to this day, and time with him was a grand experiment for how we ran the program. I was matched with Shawn when he was eleven. We met up each weekend while his mom worked, relieving his teenage sister of childcare duties. On our early talks, he expressed an interest in learning about Satan, but within a few weeks, he was asking me to take him to church. He learned about God through church services, but in his teenage years, he decided it wasn't for him. He stopped going to church, but that never damaged our friendship.

During these difficult teenage years, we usually had a drop off in kids participating in the program as they wanted to spend more time with their friends. I had an idea to invite his friends over once a week. That way I was able to learn more about his friends, and maybe even show them about God's love. During the most difficult of those teenage years, we had a group of kids over on a Friday night, consumed more pizza than was probably healthy, and played video games or watched movies. They all had a blast, and we were confident that at least on the Friday nights, they weren't getting in a lot of trouble. During this period, I was able to meet several other kids who also had a need for a mentor, and I counseled most of them at times while they grew up. Whether or not they become Christians is God's business. The bottom line is that I showed them what being a Christian really means. Our experiment worked: the kids stayed in the program longer than usual, and the other teenagers had an adult they could talk to who wasn't just interested in beer and women.

All my works of Christian service empowered me with the Spirit of God in boldness. I was able to eventually go back to William in love. I was able to preach the Gospel of Jesus Christ to the one who chased me out of the house with a shotgun. Sadly, he rejected the Gospel that night, and within six months, he also rejected life. He shot himself in a fit of rage one August afternoon. To my knowledge, he never accepted Christ.

My final word of advice to any Christian is this: You *must* find a ministry and serve God with all your heart. He has prepared a ministry for you[1], you just need to find it. Such opportunities can be found in your church or in your community. You may be called to teach in a Sunday School, or maybe you will be called to work in a soup kitchen. I advise young Christians to start by finding a ministry in the local church, but as you mature in Christ (which shouldn't take too long), start branching out into the community to share the Gospel to all the world (after all, most ministries *in* the church are usually serving Christians alone, not the community). Do not discount reaching your friends and co-workers for God. Be different—be sanctified and holy, loving all people, and when their life starts falling apart, you can counsel them. They will seek you out because of your Godly demeanor. Find your ministry, whatever it is, and serve God unapologetically with it. Let God be your guide.

---
1 Ephesians 2:10

Found by Jesus

The Sower in the Garden

January 12, 2005

As I throw this seed, I wonder what it will be
Will it grow up strong, will it know where to belong
Will it lift up eyes on the sky, and lift its name to the Most High
I look around this garden; I can't help but think so pardon
Will He grow these seeds?

Across my life my actions show, of the types of seeds I did sow
I praise the Lord for His intervention, for my death He placed into suspension
I can't help to think that I did destroy, a little girl or a little boy
I know the debt that I owe, for the tragic seeds I did sow
Will He grow these seeds?

The time I spent in the desert hard, the wanderings so long, so far
You gathered me up and placed within, pain of life, through thick and thin
I started at last to realize, that in responsibility we must live our lives
All those around us are the gardens we sow, and sometimes pray that nothing grows
Will He grow those seeds?

There came a time You called me out, I heard it so clear, as a shout
I set down the pain and sorrow, I looked ahead to tomorrow
You delivered me out of the past, all that I yearned for, at last!
You set me up and delivered a burden, and set me in Your garden
Will You grow my seeds?

I seek now to repay my debt, my heart on that is surely set
I see the growth You gave to me, will You give it to others? I will have to wait and see
What I see in the garden is pain, enough that without Your comfort, would drive me insane

I see the hearts, soiled and crying, laden with death, alone and dying
Will You grow my seeds?

My burden to love those dying souls, keeps me in You, for only You can keep me full
I see the heart that lives in denial, and I ponder the pain for a while
I see the heart in its decay, and I can only pray
In you comes the power for delivery, I can only sow the seed and wait to see.
Will You grow my seeds?

You give us the people to burden love, and we forget our hearts should be on You above
You bring in the power of Your pain, and pull us back to You again
We get too caught up in growing seeds, we forget to plant, water, and then leave
We want to take the power from You, and show You what we think we can do
Will You grow my seeds?

I see now that first child, the pain on his face, confusion mild
If he came to know through me, I would be full of unrighteous glee
But You took me out of the way, and all I could do was pray
I prayed so hard that I turned to You, and You turned and showed what You could do
You grew that seed!

I look now at the place where I am, in the garden, with a little lamb
I know beyond all doubt, enough to never pout
That You gave me evidence of his salvation, so I now see his restoration
If I see it with my own eyes, I don't know, but I may cry
You will grow that seed!

I can stop my trying hard, and I can be sure to let down my guard
I know beyond all measurable doubt, that I can get You with just a shout

Found by Jesus

I know that You are in control, the pain You allow must come to full
For out of my pain I grew so strong, and that burden does last so hard, so long
Please, Lord, grow my seeds!

I know that with pain You purify, it hurts so bad I lay down and cry
I see the pain on the children's faces, and plead to You for enduring stasis
I know that You placed me in the garden, and gave me the souls of the hardened
I know, Lord, what I must do, I must point them up toward You
Please, Lord, grow my seeds!

It is easy to come to discourage, when so desperately we want assurance
It is easy to try to change another, like a friend, lover, or a brother
We do not have the power, for only God is the great endower
Do not be weary; troubled, or toiled, For Gods plans can not be foiled
He is The Root, The Vine, The Power, under His rule, the world must cower.

Miracles and Prophecies

The most frequent questions I get about faith while talking to unbelievers center on miracles. This is not unexpected. The religious leaders in Jesus's day also asked Him about signs and wonders:

> *The Pharisees and Sadducees came up, and testing Jesus, they asked Him to show them a sign from heaven (Matthew 16:1).*

The assumption appears to be simple: show me a miracle, and I might believe in your God. The sad reality is that those whom are not called by God[1] will never believe. They will always find a way to excuse miracles, signs, and wonders as a coincidence of some kind. I want to affirm here that God is a powerful force in this world, though He tends to make His actions known clearly to those whom already know Him. This is not surprising, since the parables Jesus spoke in were also veiled truths only for the people who already know God[2]. In order to show you the power of God, I first need to educate you about a few nuances in the Christian life as it pertains to miracles versus providence, prophecy and intent. We need to understand how God works through His people today.

God is always at work. He binds the universe together by his Word[3], holding every molecule under his sovereign control. If a single molecule were ever outside of God's control, then the whole universe is outside of His control. Somewhere in this

---

1 John 6:44
2 Matthew 13:10-17
3 Colossians 1:17

mystery is an allowance for ways that glorify Him. Whether your experiences are good or bad, caused by a fallen world or human activity, God is always glorified. Be assured, this world is temporary. It's a training ground for the eternal world that is to come, and the new world will be perfect: devoid of sin, lacking negative consequences, and free from tears[1]. This new creation is for God's called and chosen people. We aren't there yet, but God is still at work presently.

Providence is the primary means that God uses to direct His will in our present time. *Providence means God is causing changes through the natural laws operating in the world.* This means that for God to heal someone, He operates through our body's natural workings or through medicine. He may cause remembrance of a past event or an inkling to look over a job application again to direct the situations of His people. These are things that God may respond to by His will or even in response to prayer. Providence is not miraculous, but it is a direct result of God working in our world. To secular people, providence looks like "good luck" but it is really just God directing his blessings for those people whom He loves[2].

A miracle is also a response God can make to the world, but rather than acting through His natural laws, a miracle suspends natural laws. "It's a miracle" is often declared when something seems beyond coincidence and possibility. A *bona fide* miracle could be declared after exhausting all scientific investigation of the supposed "miraculous". Some today declare that miracles can't happen any more. They are often well intentioned, and cite 1 Corinthians 12:8-10 to illustrate their point:

> *Love never fails; but if there are gifts of prophecy, they will be done away; if there are tongues, they will cease; if there is*

---

1 Revelation 21:1
2 Romans 8:28

knowledge, it will be done away. For we know in part and we prophesy in part; but when the perfect comes, the partial will be done away.

The idea is that when the New Testament was completed, prophecy was done away with (though they preach the merits of *knowing* the Bible.) This is a difficult and divisive discussion, but it is nevertheless worth addressing. First, we need to understand that even in the Bible, miracles were extremely rare. The three periods of explosive miracles followed Moses, then Joshua to a lesser extent, Elijah and Elisha, and Jesus and the apostles. These periods each brought explosive and powerful miracles to verify God's message. Moses was delivering God's people out of the hands of Egypt, Elijah was a powerful prophet declaring, for the first time, that God was unhappy with the failure of His people to follow His law, and Jesus ushered in the new covenant. Outside of these periods and people, we did see the occasional miracle:

Confusion of language at Babylon – Genesis 11:1-9

Balaam's donkey talked – Numbers 22:28

Samson has miraculous strength – Judges 13-16

Men of Beth-Shemoth destroyed – 1 Samuel 6:19-20

Hezekiah's Healing and sundial – 2 kings 20:7, 11

Fiery Furnace survival – Daniel 3:19-30

I didn't list any new testament miracles because all of them are centered around Jesus and the apostles. In church history, there are many suggestions of miracles. Obviously, some are forgeries, but still others are compelling enough to merit investigation. Rather than list many possible miracles starting with the ancient church fathers up to present time, William Young, a retired parish minister in the Church of Scotland wrote a compelling paper titled *Miracles in Church History* that is worth a read for anyone curious about modern miracles and how they work[1].

The point is this: The miracles which confirmed the message of God are instructive to our life and faith through the establishment of the Scriptures, but now that we have the Bible, does that mean God can't perform miracles any more? It does not. The conflict comes because many churches and Christians seek miracles and anything that looks like a miracle. They are quick to declare any such sign as a work from God, but we know that Satan also works in this way:

> *No wonder, for even Satan disguises himself as an angel of light (2 Corinthians 11:14).*

The principle is simple: miracles are rare and we shouldn't seek them, but to say God *can't* work in miracles now is short-sighted, and frankly, American. We have been so blessed with religious freedoms and opportunity in America that God waits for our faith and dedication before He will give us a taste of the miraculous, but in countries where the Bible and the Gospel is illegal, many miraculous reports have been documented. I don't want to put God in a box declaring in my humanness[2], what God can and cannot do.

Finally, we come to prophecy. A prophecy is a message from God, usually manifest through dreams or visions. They always align themselves with Scripture and generally hold a personal meaning or message. I will differentiate here between a message a person may hear now that guides their personal life and a Biblical prophecy applicable to the nation of Israel or to the establishment of the church. Those messages are done. We have the Bible, and there will not be any new prophecy meant

---

1 Young, William, *Miracles in Church History*, 1988, Churchman, vol 102/2, pg 102,
2 Job 40:1-5

for the whole church. But as people seeking and serving God, He will direct our steps. Usually He directs those steps through premonitions, though many people have experienced dreams that turned out having a prophetic nature about them.

As we have explained the various ways that God works, you can see that He usually works through providence. He can, though rarely, work through miracles. When He does work through miracles, it is never to prove who He is, but rather, it honors the faith of dedicated Christians. God usually speaks to us through the Bible, through sound counsel, and basic premonitions when we are dedicated to Him. Psalm 37:4 says,

> **Delight yourself in the Lord; And He will give you the desires of your heart.**

This means that when we are walking in His teachings and patterns, the things we want to do will honor Him, and our choices determine our steps. But occasionally, God will give us powerful messages through dreams and visions. We must be careful with those messages because they will never contradict the Scripture and they exist to bring honor to God. Anything that fails to exalt God or is out of alignment with the Scriptures is not from Him. The pattern of the Christian should be dedication to the faithful disciplines of prayer and Bible study, not seeking prophecies or miracles, but honoring God in the rare times they show up.

To this end, miracles in the modern church are often given a bad impression in many circles by the proliferation of false prophets and fake miracle workers. In one town where I lived, a local church had a regular "healing" service to entice the sick and injured from town to go for healing. Never one time did I ever see or hear anything about genuine healing. To the prophetic end, I attended a prophet's talk at a local church at the request of my pastor who sought my opinion. I watched a charismatic man sing and deal out "prophecies" that were too general to have specific meaning. It was clear he was experienced in reading people, similar to how a conman picks his target. One such prophecy he dished out told a little kid in the church that he was "very creative" and "pleased God". This wasn't a hard prophecy to dish out: the kid never stirred for the whole service and spent the whole time coloring a page in a coloring book.

The other prophecy centered around the congregation's ex-convict. The man was on parole and found Jesus in prison. He looked like an ex-con: tattooed up and down, clearly rough around the edges, but he sat in the front of the church. The prophet dished out his message: "You led a hard life, but you are finally on a good track and following God with all your heart." This general message looks impressive when viewed without a critical eye. Maybe the prophet should have told him to be careful, for only a week after completing his parole, he was back to his old ways.

Not withstanding the falsities which many of us often observe in the Christian world, have I ever witnessed miracles or visions? Yes, I have.

The event we will call a miracle centered around a young girl in our church. She was actually the younger sister of the boy who I prayed for a Christian influence to come into his life, and soon after, his mom had become a Christian. He had a younger sister and they were playing on a trampoline. The girl took a blow to the head and lost all vision out of one of her eyes. She was taken to doctors and specialists who performed a battery of tests, finally concluding that her vision loss was likely permanent.

Never giving up hope, this young Christian brought her daughter before our church for a special prayer meeting (no, this was not a church that conducts the dubious "healing" services). We prayed over the girl and besought God that He may restore her sight. Suddenly one day, about a week later, the girl's vision miraculously was restored. The doctors performed another batch of tests and determined that nothing natural or medical helped this girl receive her sight. It was declared by the doctors a miraculous event.

Hearing that story, any non-believer can find a way to justify the event as some fluke of coincidence. And that is often how we find miracles in our lives. They never prove who God is, but they may work in people who have reached out to Him and believed He would respond. Remember that belief is the chief factor, never evidence. Even Jesus was prevented from many miracles in His home town because the people wouldn't believe:

> Jesus said to them, "A prophet is not without honor except in his hometown and among his own relatives and in his own household." And He could do no miracle there except that He laid His hands on a few sick people and healed them (Mark 6:4-5).

Prophecy is also rare, but I have a prophetic experience that confirms for me the existence, power, and voice of God. Like all modern prophecy, it was not a message to be added to the pages of the Bible, for the canon of Scripture is complete. Though it was a message delivered to me by God for His glorification and the exhortation of a wavering believer.

On this day, I lay in bed somewhere between awake and asleep when dreams are the most vivid. I had the vision of a kid, a young boy on the verge of adolescence, a boy I recognized, but didn't know. In the vision, the boy was toying with sexual immorality, impurity, and he struggled. The vision also made it known that he was a kid a great distance away. I jolted awake in the vision, the sights burned on my mind, but I didn't understand what it meant. I filed it away like Mary, treasuring in her heart the visions spoken to her by the shepherds on the night Jesus was born[1].

The most intriguing part of the vision was the distance. I loved where I lived and I didn't have any desire, or even plans, to move. God, however, started pulling strings in the background. One by one, opportunities to work crumbled to dust as I tried to keep my life situation where it was. One by one, He closed doors and then opened up an opportunity to move thousands of miles away. He provided a place to live and steady work.

Once the move was complete, God sent work in His service as well. I took several positions in ministry, which included mentoring one boy that I had the intense feeling was the one in the vision. *Had God really brought me across the county for this purpose?* I asked myself. It was too weird for me to consider, yet still I filed away the event in my mind.

A number of years passed and my relationship with the boy grew to the point where he trusted me with his deeper secrets, and one of those secrets included an addiction to pornography. Instantly the vision flashed before my mind, and I took a sticky note, writing a date on it and sealing the note in an envelope. It sat sealed on the table the night before the young man was coming over to tell me the whole story. He unfolded an addiction that fostered itself through a few years. He told me about what drove his curiosity to look at such images, and he told me the date that he first looked at them. Mean while, he fiddled with the envelope; it was the only thing on the table for nervous and fidgeting hands.

"Open that envelope," I ordered.

---

[1] Luke 2:19

He opened it up and looked at the sticky note. His jaw dropped to the table, his eyes darting before the note and my eyes. The date on the note matched, to the night, when he first looked at the vile images that now tormented his conscience. God had given me the vision of his sin on the very night he partook of it!

From thousands of miles away, God gave me a vision of a boy who was starting down a road of sexual addiction. He ordered my life to move when I had no plans to do so, and he brought this exact kid in the visions into my mentorship. He directed our relationship to grow to the point of trust, and used that vision to clarify His own role in our lives.

From this powerful vision, it gave the final confirmation to this young man that God *is* real and that He is involved in our life. Through prayer, God's confirmation, and a few plans of action, he used the vision to exhort a young believer into a real faith. As of this writing, the young man has grown close to God and has not looked at pornographic material since.

We see in this prophecy that God worked a vision to bring two people closer confirmation of His existence and power. He used it to exhort both parties to walk closer with God, directed us both into His word, and brought glory to His name by empowering us to walk closer with Him. That is modern day prophecy in action.

Though You Slay Me

Some people will say that coming to Jesus makes everything better. I'm not sure where they got that idea. The Bible certainly doesn't promise us sunshine and roses as we walk our life with Jesus. In fact, the Bible actually paints the opposite picture:

> But be on your guard; for they will deliver you to the courts, and you will be flogged in the synagogues, and you will stand before governors and kings for My sake, as a testimony to them. The gospel must first be preached to all the nations. When they arrest you and hand you over, do not worry beforehand about what you are to say, but say whatever is given you in that hour; for it is not you who speak, but it is the Holy Spirit. Brother will betray brother to death, and a father his child; and children will rise up against parents and have them put to death. You will be hated by all because of My name, but the one who endures to the end, he will be saved (Mark 13:9-13).

If we live our lives with our mind on the Gospel, we will lose friends. Our family will think we're nuts, and if we stick to the Scripture, the world will eventually come against us. Just ask the baker who wouldn't bake a custom wedding cake for a homosexual couple! Of course, these are some of the things we experience as we live boldly for the Lord, which is what we always need to do.

Even outside of our obligations to the Gospel, we are still not promised a life free from trouble. Sure, we'll always have the peace of Christ, and we can rest in that peace[1]. But we live in a

---
1 Matthew 11:30

fallen world where bad things sometime happen. Job's life gives us an example of calamity waiting in the wings:

> A messenger came to Job and said, "The oxen were plowing and the donkeys feeding beside them, and the Sabeans attacked and took them. They also slew the servants with the edge of the sword, and I alone have escaped to tell you." While he was still speaking, another also came and said, "The fire of God fell from heaven and burned up the sheep and the servants and consumed them, and I alone have escaped to tell you." While he was still speaking, another also came and said, "The Chaldeans formed three bands and made a raid on the camels and took them and slew the servants with the edge of the sword, and I alone have escaped to tell you." While he was still speaking, another also came and said, "Your sons and your daughters were eating and drinking wine in their oldest brother's house, and behold, a great wind came from across the wilderness and struck the four corners of the house, and it fell on the young people and they died, and I alone have escaped to tell you (Job 1:14-19).

These trials all came about because God tested Job when Satan said that the man only praised the Lord because of his blessings. In the next chapter, Satan was also allowed to take Job's health away. He still praised God even though his wife counseled him to curse God and die. He wouldn't. He chose to accept both good and bad from God[1]. The point isn't that every bad thing that happens in our life is because God and the Devil are cosmically gambling. More important than the big problems we face in life, is the bigger God we can turn to, even when what He is doing makes no earthly sense to us from our perspectives. Job called out with a proclamation of real faith:

> *Though He slay me, I will hope in Him.*
> *Nevertheless I will argue my ways before Him.*
> *(Job 13:15)*

---

1 Job 2:9-10

All Christians need to learn this lesson. We can't praise God when good things come into our life and turn away from Him at the slightest hint of trouble. All of us will go through periods of personal tribulation. Perhaps God ordains it to test our faith to determine if we are really worthy to receive the crown of life promised to those who persevere[1]. Hopefully my story of personal tribulation can help strengthen others, so I gladly tell it. Again, these stories of trials happened after I was a new creation and saved by God.

Probably one of the first major tests I encountered was a test about walking the fine line between faithfulness to family, as abusive as they were, and learning to set my own boundaries. The pressure was mounting in my professional life as I was beginning the process of preparing for my doctoral defense and starting my first professorship at the same time.

I moved to a tiny town on the edge of our county in Pennsylvania so half the week I could return to my research lab to finalize experiments and the other half of the time I could travel the opposite direction to teach. The event happened on orientation day. I was handed my ID card and keys to my first academic office. I had arrived at the big time. I was gathering my things, sitting at my new desk and planning my first few days of class when the phone rang. I heard frantic yelling on the other end of the line, demanding to know where I was.

"At my new job," I said, slightly confused. *Did I miss an appointment?* I thought to myself, but I didn't have time.

"We left messages! Get over here!" My brother demanded. The phone went dead.

---

[1] James 1·12

I flipped open the phone and noticed the message indicating several voice mails. They were frantic and disjointed, but apparently, William had snapped and starting waving his gun around aggressively. He pointed it to my moms head, then turned it to himself and fired right in front of my mother. He died instantly on the front porch in some argument over the deep freezer.

I sent a quick email from my new faculty email address; the first faculty email I would send informing everyone in the department of a death that I had to attend to. I never even returned home, I just took the few things I had with me and jumped on the interstate heading back to the north east. I stopped at my cousins house back in the town where the cows out number the people three to one, and stayed there to coax my mother not to return home, but to come over there to stay for a few days.

This was a true test of my faithfulness to family. I still wasn't on good speaking terms with them, but I saw the need to get my mother out of the house where William killed himself. I stayed there for a few days, but finally spoke with my aunt that I had to return to my new job. I promised to keep in touch, and I made it out the following week for the funeral.

This wasn't the first vicarious suicide I experienced in life, but God had worked in my heart. This was the man that I once wrote in my journal that I wanted to kill him. If ever I hated anyone, it was William. Shortly before his death I was able to share the Gospel with him. As rough as our relationship was, I have peace that I did all I could have done to introduce him to God. This was not a good situation, but God was indeed faithful in getting me through the mess.

Things were mostly smooth for a few years, but even looking back now, I still can't place when the deeper trials really began.

Though You Slay Me

Maybe it was the 2007 market crash that put a strain on workers, property values, and relationships. Maybe it started later when I decided I was going to try to make it on my own in this world without being beholden to a company issuing me a solid paycheck. I can assume the trials began while I was living out west. At first, everything was awesome. I had joined a good church and had a good job. My debt was being weaned into near non-existence, and I was working some excellent ministries on multiple fronts.

Somewhere in that joy, something dark was just out of reach. I made the decision to leave my job. For a while, everything ran smoothly, and then I seemed to hit multiple road bumps all at once. First, client work entered a dry spell causing my resources to run thin. As hard as I tried, it was like every proposal fell into a pit. I was forced to cut back dramatically on spending (not that I was ever a big spender anyway). Eventually the money completely ran out and I had to decide if I could short sell my house, cash out all my retirement, or both at the same time.

Right at this critical juncture, I lost a very dear friend, a kid who was like a son to me. I was toying with moving back to the east, and the loss of my friend pushed me over the edge – I couldn't bare to go through town seeing all the places we hung out together. I cashed out the retirement to keep the house afloat and fund moving back east while I attempted to sell the property. I packed my Buick full of my most important possessions and started the two-thousand mile trip back to the east. I had a place to stay for a month while a more permanent apartment opened up in town. I arrived only to find that the house didn't have any cell reception and no options for the Internet. This situation wasn't what I needed for working a home-based web company.

The morning after I arrived at the house I went out to start up the car to go to church, but the car wouldn't budge. The engine had blown up after the long journey. It was, I guess, only by God's grace that it blew in the parking lot rather than somewhere a midst the frozen Iowan corn fields. But still, I was stranded here without a way to work, a car, losing my house, and cashing out retirement just to eat. I had truly hit the very bottom. I was faithful to God in every way possible, yet still, I suffered.

Life is not always good to us. Sometimes God needs to prune away the distractions around us to bring about more faithful presence in His arms. Jesus teaches us such things in John 15:

> *Every branch in Me that does not bear fruit, He takes away; and every branch that bears fruit, He prunes it so that it may bear more fruit (vs 2).*

> *My Father is glorified by this, that you bear much fruit, and so prove to be My disciples (vs 8).*

With all the things I have seen God do in this world, I was not ready to walk away from Him just because things got tough. He could take everything away, and still I would praise Him. Though He take my friends, and my house, and my car, and my work, I will not run from Him, nor will I abandon Him. Jesus's own disciples said it best:

> *Lord, to whom shall we go? You have words of eternal life (John 6:68).*

I end this chapter repeating the words of Job:

> *Though He slay me, I will hope in Him.*
> *Nevertheless I will argue my ways before Him.*
> *(Job 13:15)*

A Tale of Two Lifestyles

Having lived half my life as an atheist and the other as a Christian, I have some perspective on the consequences of each lifestyle. As you may have deduced, having made it this far in my journey, I didn't have a wonderful upbringing. I don't want to paint a picture that every kid from an atheist home had the same struggles I suffered. Nor is it accurate to say that being raised in a Christian home keeps a child safe from abuse and dysfunction. At the center, however, is the response to the world around us. True Christianity gives us a new life and worldview. We cannot proclaim to be a Christian and ignore all that Jesus and the Bible tells us. All our upbringings give us perspective through the worldviews: what is acceptable, how do we respond to tragedy, is there justice in our cruel world? My conversion to Christianity changed my outlook on life, and, that always changes our reaction to the world around us.

Presently, I want to give perspective about my life through my various struggles and conquests, how I responded as an atheist adult, and how similar situations are handled now. For our first example, let's revisit the sexual sins in my past. My intent was to "save myself" for marriage. For some reason this was important to me, though I couldn't explain a reason for such blatant morality in the midst of my filthy mind. On the night I first "knew" Annie, I loved every bit of pleasure in the midst of the act. Like most college-aged kids, hormones could overwhelm my rational thought, even though I spent a whole evening mediating over my decisions and deciding, in my own power, to resist any sexual advances. But when a naked woman commands a man, hormones wipe out all rationalization. Sexual contact was a forgone conclusion by merit of a foolish midnight meeting[1].

The brief moment of pleasure was juxtaposed with a sleepless night. I had disobeyed my conscience, and my inner voice screamed my failures to my mind. When I finally silenced it with excuses like, *but what if I never marry, I might never have this opportunity again.* Only a second of peace passed by before the next concern bounded into my mind, hours too late to be useful: *What if I got her pregnant?* There were no specific precautions, and in the words of my biochemistry professor: "Of course you know what happens when people have sex!" The voices were not over. Next was the question of disease. Hundreds of sexually transmitted diseases have been discovered, and it was possible I may have just picked one up. *No*, I said to myself, *Annie is more careful than that...right?* I didn't know, I just presumed. The first voice came back and these three concerns kept me up nearly until dawn as I attempted to sleep on Annie's couch. I rejected the opportunity to sleep with her in bed.

The morning came too fast, and I woke up a failure to myself. Not only did I crumble under my supposed "conquest", but our friendship crumbled as well. Once we were good friends, we studied, and had good, clean fun, but now, having pried open the door to fornication, every meeting ended in lust. Even my juxtaposed emotions wavered between ecstasy and horror, but the conscience became numb to sex. As Pink Floyd wrote:

> *Day after Day, Love Turns Grey*
> *Like the Skin on a Dying Man*

---

[1] Proverbs 7

A Tale of Two Lifestyles

> And Night after Night, We pretend it's all right
> But I have grown older, And you have grown colder
> And nothing is very much fun, Anymore

I experienced this decay as my personal goals were lost to a blind autopilot of doing things that I actually hated, not for the moment of pleasure, but for the way it pricked my conscience, for I never had feelings of love for this woman.

After becoming a Christian and growing in my faith, I decided that I needed to put an end to any future meetings with Annie. On the day I gave this sin to Christ and sought His forgiveness, I was instantly set free[1]. Not only did God give me the power to resist future sexual temptations (and I had more than one test), but He also finally gave me peace of mind and a strategy to minimize temptation: Stop engaging with sexually explicit films and music. Our media entertainment seriously impacts how we respond to temptations. So having failed in my task of sexual purity, only God was able to restore my peace. He was the one person who could make my conscience quiet again.

Another great lesson on the shifting worldview of a believer was education. After my radical personal change in the tenth grade, I was undeniably unstoppable in the academic sense. While I started high school in the nebulous "learning lab," I ended with presidential honors for improvement, even taking on extracurricular subjects in my personal time. By the time I finished high school I was studying Latin, psychology, natural medicines, herbology, and I loved every minute of it. Into college, I read two complete biochemistry textbooks *prior* to taking the class and fit in an advanced study of nuclear chemistry during the Christmas break in my senior year. The college noticed my academic achievements and made me the live-in science tutor for the hall of science majors.

---

[1] 1 John 1:9

I saw the doors opening up, and a perfect career of cash-filled positions were waiting for me. My future was so bright that I thought I was emanating the light from my academic perfection. I created my own destiny. In the words of William Ernest Henley, I was *the master of my fate, the captain of my soul*. When I was a god unto myself, I also boasted with a pride that pushed people away. I didn't desire friends so much as I desired learning new things, because education was my ticket out of the hell I was raised in.

A looming contradiction lurked at the edge of my mind. The more I learned, the more I knew, but nothing I ever learned helped me in the emotional sense. The baggage of my past kept clinging to me, no matter how much I attempted to suppress it with more work and education. I even sought to learn, to understand human emotion. I explored myself to see why I was held back, and the answer was always just beyond me. It was that desire to break free of my past, to launch into the future that peaked my attention on that day Jesus conquered me.

On that day, I laid before Jesus my past. He showed me that I wasn't a passive victim, but an active sinner in my own life. I had the sense that I needed to let that sin go. As I handed it to Him, he gave me a peace that I never experienced before. It was like Jesus whispered in my ear, "I was with you when those people hurt you...and I was with you when you hurt people back." The secret that I remained illusive in all my learning was that I needed to accept my own pride and responsibility. I needed to turn my back on the ways I was hurt and how I hurt others. I needed to embrace who He was. The final days of giving up that wretched past occurred just before He launched me into that first VBS program. The education didn't help me in my life, and we will never reach the end of knowledge[1]. The

---

[1] Ecclesiastes 12·12

A Tale of Two Lifestyles

endpoint of man is to give up our life to God, and serve Him[2]. Knowing Jesus is all the knowing we need to have in order to live a fulfilled life. This lesson came not from books, but from God, Himself.

As He taught me, he also had to change my mind about people. When you come from a background such as mine, trust doesn't come easily. I grew up suspicious of everyone. I had very few friends, and frankly, I liked it that way. A few of my friends over the years betrayed me, and I saw that as the whole world being against me (though that is normal over the course of life, I didn't know it). As I was often used for other people's satisfaction and then discarded at the end of the day, I started holding people aloof. In middle school, the bullies pushed me into an emotional corner, but by high school, I broke out by being cruel. I didn't know it until after my high school graduation, but my brother told me that most of the school grew to fear me. Perhaps it was that time I showed a girl my pen and explained in excruciating detail how I would maim her face with it. While I wasn't a violent person, the persona of such violence served me well as I sought to distance myself from everyone.

In college, I let down my guard a bit as I was forced to live in the residence halls. I didn't have a choice but to mingle since I was paid to interact with people. I learned how to put on a social front that could help someone with their science without developing relationships. The few people that were able to get close, like Annie, more often than not asked more of me than I was willing to give. All except Dr. Daniels. He had something about himself that seemed to give without taking. This interesting contrast to the other people I interacted with gave me pause to think. I felt like I could actually be myself around him without putting up my guard. The end of it all: I

---

[2] Ecclesiastes 12:13

hated people, and I grew to love loneliness, even though it often plunged me into some form of depression.

Becoming a Christian changed my disposition toward people. After my intense encounter with Jesus, I started actually being nice to others. I didn't push folks away so quickly, and I even started putting a bit of book learning on the back burner to just spend some evenings with people engaging in games, movies, or conversation.

I recognized the difference Dr. Daniels had to the rest of the world. He knew this Jesus, of whom I now belonged, and that infused my soul with a sudden care for other people that was foreign to me on prior days. My experience turned from depression and hatred to a calm caring. As I grew more in Christ, I enjoyed going to more Bible classes at church, spending time at some of the Christian gatherings like the picnics and fellowship times. These people were not out to hurt me, and I eventually learned to be myself, allowing people to learn who I really was. The community that exists around the church is the lifeblood of Christ, and we should participate when we can. Ultimately, my life before and after being a Christian could not be any more different when considering my interactions and joys of being with people, introvert though I still am.

Ultimately, the chief difference between my two lifestyles was the presence and absence of God. When I lived without looking to a God, life took on a different meaning. No one waited in the wings keeping an eye on me. The things that happened to me were a result of people wanting to do me harm, my own failure to protect myself, or any combination thereof. This means life without God is a life of paranoid caution. I always looked out for myself because no one else would look out for me on earth or in heaven. I had to make every opportunity happen because if I didn't create my own opportunity, life itself would pass me by. Life without God is a life with the weight of the world on your shoulders. For sure, this weight is what pushes most people to consume drugs and alcohol. It causes most people to live life for the pleasure of weekends, but still clench the weight of the world between their fingers. This drives some people mad, and makes others neurotic academics, like myself. There is never a release unless it is intentional, like the soma in *Brave New World*, we look to our personal worlds bravely, or cowering in fear that things may spin out of control at any moment in time.

After I met Jesus, all that changed. Now my worldview included a powerful and sovereign God who is able to bend the world to the favor of those who love Him[1]. A God who loves me is a God who cares. A God who is powerful is a God who can protect me, even when I am not sure how best to protect myself. The contrast in my personal outlook on life was paramount. My life before Christ was paranoid, hateful, suspicious. That is not a way to spend time on earth. But after Christ, a peace overcame me that allowed me to let down my hair in the presence of others. I set down the suspicions and learned that I could actually trust some people, particularly those of God's household.

It's fair to say that my negative and pessimistic attitude as a non-believer gave way to a peace and a comfort that I had only ever dreamed of. God did change every part of my life. He saw fit to instantly remove some sin. He gave me instruction on how to personally conquer other transgressions. Not that I am the perfection of positive attitude, but the fact I no longer have to be the master of my fate and the captain of my soul is enough to take the great pressures off my shoulders. What did Jesus say:

---

[1] Romans 8:28

Found by Jesus

Come to Me, all who are weary and heavy-laden, and I will give you rest. Take My yoke upon you and learn from Me, for I am gentle and humble in heart, and you will find rest for your souls. For My yoke is easy and My burden is light (Matthew 11:28-30).

Scripture Index

New Testament..........................
- 1 Corinthians 12...........................248
- 1 Corinthians 15..................44, 65, 73
- 1 John 1....................................237, 265
- 2 Corinthians 11...........................250
- 2 Corinthians 5.....................227, 237
- Colossians 1..................................247
- Ephesians 2............................237, 243
- Ephesians 4..................................231
- Galatians 6.....................................72
- Hebrews 13....................................71
- James 1...................................44, 259
- James 3..239
- James 4..230
- James 5..238
- John 14..233
- John 15.................................233, 262
- John 6.......................238, 247, 262
- John 8..237
- Luke 12..240
- Mark 13..257
- Mark 6..253
- Matthew 10....................................42
- Matthew 11............................257, 270
- Matthew 13..................................247
- Matthew 16..................................247
- Matthew 18..................................241
- Matthew 28..................................241
- Matthew 7......................................99
- Philippians 1................................227
- Philippians 4................................233

- Revelation 21...............................248
- Revelation 22...............................230
- Revelation 3.................................230
- Romans 12.......................231p., 237
- Romans 3......................................238
- Romans 7....................135, 159, 195
- Romans 8....................151, 248, 269

Old Testament...........................
- 1 Samuel 6....................................249
- 2 Chronicles 34............................232
- Daniel 3...249
- Deuteronomy 21.............................73
- Ecclesiastes 10..............................151
- Ecclesiastes 12...........................266p.
- Ecclesiastes 4..................................21
- Genesis 11.....................................249
- Genesis 22....................................232
- Isaiah 65.......................................215
- Jeremiah 31............................42, 146
- Job 13...................................258, 262
- Job 15...13
- Job 40...250
- Judges 13......................................249
- Numbers 22.................................249
- Proverbs 12.....................................70
- Proverbs 15..............................59, 73
- Proverbs 17....................................17
- Proverbs 25....................................20
- Proverbs 29....................................10
- Proverbs 5..7
- Proverbs 7............................197, 264

I AM not amused

ISBN:
978-1-7325696-2-1 (s)
978-1-7325696-3-8 (e)

Does your entertainment honor God?

Happy Hellidays

ISBN:
978-1-7325696-6-9 (s)
978-1-7325696-7-6 (e)

How can you honor God when celebrating holidays?

Josiah's Sanctification

ISBN:
978-1-732569645 (s)
978-1-7325696-5-2 (e)

What can you learn about Sanctification from an ancient king?

www.ingramcontent.com/pod-product-compliance
Lightning Source LLC
Chambersburg PA
CBHW060351080526
44583CB00012B/270